CHILDREN WHO RULED THE WORLD

True Stories Out of Egypt, China, England, France, and Russia

Other books by Joe Kraus:

Alive in the Desert:
The Complete Guide For
Desert Recreation and Survival

Staying Alive in the Desert:
The Complete Guide
For Desert Survival
(this is the 2017 revised edition)

Tales from the Deep:
The Life and Times of the USS Manatee
And It's Always Ready
and Sometimes Willing Crew

The Famous & Successful:
Their Advice for All of Us
(Co-written with Ron Stovall)

Desert Rats
They Came With a Pick,
a Shovel and a Dream

Scheduled for release shortly:

Autograph Collecting:
Why we're Doing It and How
You Can Join Us in the Fun

They Went That-A-Way:
Odd, Funny & Sad Stories
Of America's Wild West

CHILDREN WHO RULED THE WORLD

True Stories Out of Egypt, China, England, France, and Russia

The remarkably true account of young children who woke up one morning to find themselves rulers of their countries. Now, instead of spending the day at school or playing with their friends, they faced not only riots in their streets and invading armies at their borders, but the most dangerous threats of all: brothers and sisters, uncles and cousins – all members, in fact, of their own family.

By Joe Kraus

Celebrity Galleries
P.O. Box 55328
Stockton, California 95205

Children Who Ruled The World:
True Stories Out of Egypt, China,
England, France, and Russia
Copyright 2017 by Joe Kraus

ISBN-13: 978-0998632391 (Celebrity Galleries)
ISBN-10: 0998632392

Library of Congress Control Number (LCCN) 2017915533

Printed in the United States of America
Celebrity Galleries, P.O. Box 55328, Stockton, CA 95205
(209) 473-0570 celebritygalleries@sbcglobal.net

TABLE OF CONTENTS

*   *   *

SPECIAL THANKS

First, I would like to thank my wife Karren Kraus for her patience, her support, and the taking on of other duties while this book was created. I appreciate also my oldest daughter Heidi Delaney for her work in putting the words and illustrations into book format.

Much appreciation goes out to Mark Meyer who has proofread this book and all but one of my books to date. Artist R. L. Sather and creative director Rob Sturtz worked with me here for the first time. I want to thank them for their instrumental work in creating the front cover design.

Finally, I can't say enough for the assistance of Edward Johanneck. For this book in particular I want to thank him for his creative work on the back cover, for his technical support, and his advice from the beginning of this and other book projects.

Conway castle (above) and Penrhyn castle
in the United Kingdom as they look today.

INTRODUCTION

WHAT IS THIS BOOK ABOUT? This is a true account of children under the age of fourteen who became kings or rulers of their country. It centers on their childhood years during which they ruled their nation. It tells of their powers, what they did with these powers, and how their rule affected their nation.

WHY WAS THIS BOOK WRITTEN? As a youngster I used to dream about how it would be to be a king and have my own castle. As an adult I discovered in reading history that there were cases when young boys and girls were kings and queens. I wanted to know more about them and what they did. Because there was no book on the subject I decided the only way I was ever to get a better understanding was to do the research and write the book myself.

WHY WAS THE AGE OF FOURTEEN PICKED? In most countries a child isn't considered an adult until the age of eighteen. But cars can be driven when one reaches the age of sixteen. And in many areas teens are allowed to work, even get married in some cases, at the age of fourteen. Now, many adults don't consider a kid fully capable at fourteen to do much of anything. Ask any fourteen-year-old, however, and you get a different story. They believe they can handle almost any emergency. We have taken their word for it. So, fourteen it is.

WHAT IS THIS BOOK TRYING TO ACCOM-PLISH? Few people realize there were children who ruled the world. This is only natural because it is only casually mentioned in historical works. I wanted not only to point out that such situations existed, but what happened to these child rulers and their nations during that time. I also wanted to show how they handled their situation. Were any less capable than the adults ruling the world in their time or even the adults ruling today?

SO THERE WERE CHILD RULERS. BUT WEREN'T OTHERS RULING IN THEIR NAME? Yes, in most situations this was the case, but quite often they had a great deal to say and did. In cases where others ruled in their name, the king came into his own usually by the time he was twelve years old – still remarkably young in any society. In some cases age wasn't as much of a factor as demonstrating that he or she was up to the task.

WHY JUST FIVE COUNTRIES AND WHY THESE PARTICULAR ONES? There were a few other nations which in ancient times were ruled for a brief time by one or more children. In most of these cases little is known of what transpired. Five countries, however, were key. These were Egypt, China, England, France, and Russia. Here I decided to include every one of the child rulers in those countries, listing what we know of each ruler who served while under the age of fourteen.

WHY ARE THERE FEW GIRL RULERS IN THIS BOOK? While there were a few girl rulers such as Christina of Sweden and Mary Queen of Scots, much has already been written about both rulers. Christina, while she was designated the queen at an early age, didn't actually start ruling until she was eighteen. Mary, on the other hand, spent most of her childhood in France while Scotland was ruled by regents. Nevertheless, neither Sweden nor Scotland were among the countries that were selected as representative. Among the five nations that were selected, there were no female rulers under the age of fourteen. The only exception was Cleopatra who ruled only jointly with her brother and then not until she was thirteen. Her story is included as part of the later Ptolemy kings.

IS THIS A HISTORY BOOK IN THAT IT TELLS THE WHOLE STORY OF THESE INDIVIDUALS? This book covers mostly the childhood years of these individuals and only sparingly includes later accomplishments. It was determined that this was the only way this book could stay within the lines it was written.

DO WE KNOW HOW THESE CHILDREN ACTUALLY FELT ABOUT THEIR SITUATION? It would be great if we did. Those around them at the time seemed to only record accomplishments or failures, not any inner thoughts of the kings when they were young. Even close friends who lived in those times and had personal dealings with these kings weren't privy to these things. The only way we would know about their inner thoughts would be if any left journals or diaries and actually admitted to their inner thoughts. This didn't happen most likely due to the fact they had more pressing problems. And the most important of these was to survive the moment.

HOW MUCH DO WE REALLY KNOW ABOUT THESE RULERS CHILDHOODS? In some cases very little is known particularly those who ruled Egypt and China. With others however we know much more.

ABOUT THE PHOTOS: In many cases artists never drew likeliness of the young rulers while they were children. As a result we had to use the artist rendering of the ruler as an adult.

EGYPT TODAY

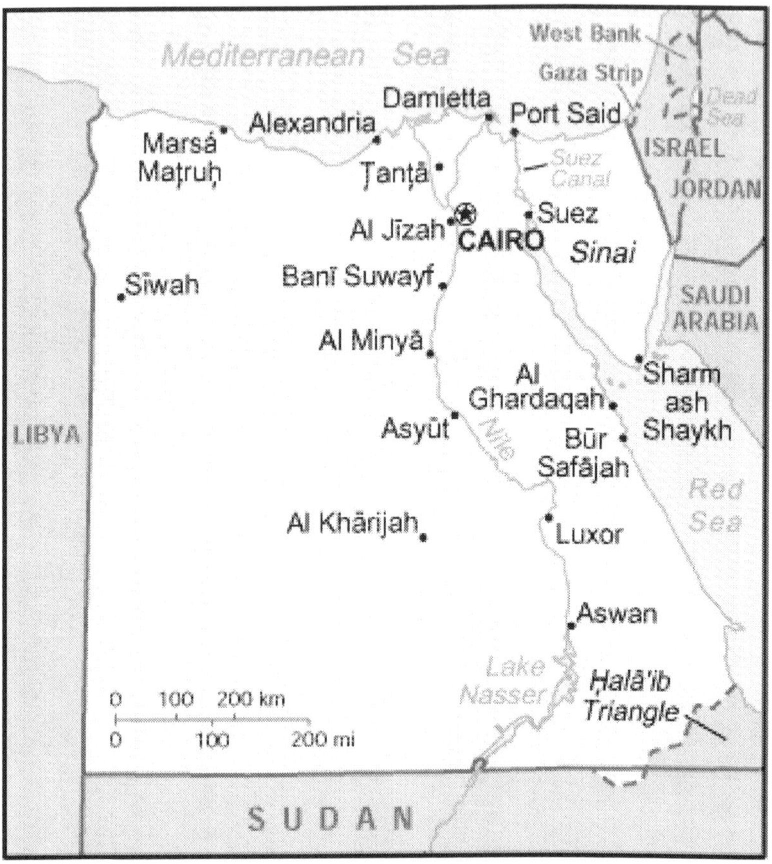

Mediterranean Sea
West Bank
Gaza Strip
Dead Sea
Damietta
Port Said
Alexandria
Marsá Maṭruḥ
Ṭanṭā
Suez Canal
ISRAEL
JORDAN
Suez
Al Jīzah
CAIRO
Sinai
Sīwah
Banī Suwayf
SAUDI ARABIA
Al Minyā
Sharm ash Shaykh
Al Ghardaqah
LIBYA
Asyūt
Nile
Būr Safājah
Red Sea
Al Khārijah
Luxor
Aswan
Lake Nasser
Ḥalā'ib Triangle
0 100 200 km
0 100 200 mi
SUDAN

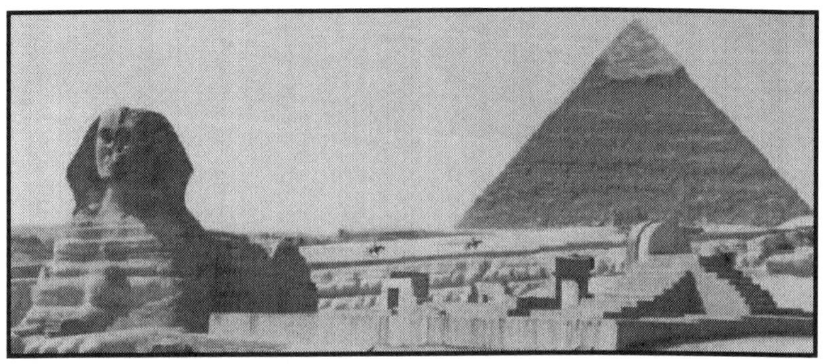

CHAPTER 1
EGYPT

Egypt is probably the most mysterious and most fascinating of all the countries of the ancient world. For, while the earliest cities were in Mesopotamia, the first great kingdom of the ancient world was in Egypt. Here the supreme authority was the king who was deemed incomparably greater than any of his subjects. He was, it was said, on intimate terms with the gods. The king preserved the well-being of Egypt and in return Egypt gave him wealth, power, and as far as it could, immortality.

It was in Egypt that the world had its first exposure to child rulers. Here the very young took on the reins of government for the first time. They made mistakes. They accomplished things. In the end the experience of these young rulers in Egypt could have become a model by which others in similar situations could follow. That didn't happen because in most cases the child rulers to come had little, if any, knowledge of the child rulers that preceded them.

Alabaster statue of Pepi II with his mother.

Pepi II Neferkare
(2284-2216 BC)
He still holds
a world record

It was more than 2,000 years before the birth of Christ when Pepi II ruled as king in Egypt. He was just six years old when he ascended to the throne of the most powerful kingdom in the world at that time. Although he was not necessarily a bad king, Pepi II did pose a great deal of hardship on Egypt.

Because of his age, a great amount of power, power that should have remained solely with the king, went to ministers, those who ruled the nation in the king's name. Not only was this power hard to regain once it had been allotted to others, but Pepi II was just too young to know if these ministers were governing wisely or not.

But just as there was a problem with his youth, years later there was also a problem with his old age. Pepi II currently has the distinction of holding the record of the longest reign of any monarch in the world. Beginning his reign in 2272 BC at the age of six, his years on the throne of Egypt lasted a total of 91 years. In those final years he was old and weak. He would have been nothing more than a shadow of himself sitting in his palace waiting to die. In his last years his feeble fingers must have let go of the reins of government altogether. And once again court ministers took over the day to day operations of his country.

What all of this meant for Egypt was a general weakening of the king's power. When Pepi II died in 2216 BC no one king could any longer exert absolute power over these ministers, who had by this time established a strong influence over government policies.

Because it was so very long ago and because records were not kept as they are today, we don't know much about the boyhood years of Pepi II. One story, however, did survive.

It tells the story of Pepi II when he was about eight years old and his eagerness to see a dwarf (pygmy). When the boy learned that one of his ministers had just returned from a foreign expedition in which he brought back a dwarf, he wrote his minister a letter. The actual content of the letter was found inscribed on the walls of the minister's tomb. It reads:

"Thou hast said in this thy letter that thou hast brought a dwarf of the dances of the God from the land of the Blessed

Spirits, like to the dwarf which the divine chancellor Baurded brought from Funt in the time of Assa... Each year thou doest the pleasure and desire of thy lord; thy sleeping and thy waking hours are devoted to the performance of that which thy lord desires, praises and commands. His majesty will do thee many excellent honors to the glory of thy son's son forever."

The boy king then issues orders that the minister is to bring down the dwarf at once by boat. The letter continues: "If he embarks with thee on a ship, let good people be behind him on the two sides of the ship to guard him from falling into the water; and when he is lying down at night, let good people lie behind him in his tent, and inspect him ten times in the night. My Majesty desires to see this dwarf more than the products of the mines and of Punt; and if thou comest to the palace and this dwarf is with thee alive and well, my Majesty will do for thee more than was done for the divine chancellor Baurded in the time of Assa, according to the disposition of the heart of my Majesty to see this dwarf..."

As the days, weeks, and months went by, the dwarf became a favorite of the king. The boy thought so very highly of him that in later life he gave him one of his own daughters in marriage. He was made custodian of the king's wardrobe. And when finally the dwarf died, he was buried honorably adjacent to Pepi II's pyramid.

Ruins of the pyramid complex of Pepi II.

Thutmose III likeness in Luxor Museum, Cairo Egypt

Thuthmose III (1481-1425 BC)
It was said he was chosen by the gods

Thutmose III was Egypt's mightiest ruler and the builder of the first real empire that the world has ever known. Reigning in Egypt close to 1,500 years before the birth of Christ, Thutmose III was pharaoh when the baby Moses was found in the bulrushes. But, like some of the pharaohs who would rule after him, his political achievements are records of murder and tyranny.

What Thutmose III was, however, was a great administrator. He disliked corrupt officials and he proved himself ruthless in eliminating this great public evil. He developed his nation's resources, extended its frontiers, and maintained order by suppressing without mercy any hint of conspiracies or revolts among his subjects.

The pharaoh's rise to stardom was not without his share of problems. But, unlike other rulers in history that were often too weak to overcome the challenges, Thutmose III decided that as pharaoh he would rule alone and he would not be influenced by those about him. Even the mighty Queen Hatshepsut, his brilliant and ambitious stepmother, was overpowered in the end.

For Thutmose III all of this started when he was but ten years old. His father, Thutmose II had just died. The burning issue in all of Egypt was who would be proclaimed pharaoh. Only a prince born by the chief royal consort had the right to the throne. There was no such prince. The pharaoh and Queen Hatshepsut had only daughters.

The boy, later to be proclaimed Thutmose III, was the male offspring of Thutmose II and a harem woman named Iris. As the son of a harem woman he would not normally ascend to the throne. A "miracle" was needed and that is just what the temple priests had in mind. Their plan was to maintain order and to give official sanction to a new pharaoh. Their opportunity came during a temple ceremony when the temple courts were filled with worshipful throngs. Among them was this boy who at that time was studying to become a priest.

When the ceremony began, several priests entered the temple, carrying in a golden chair with a large image of the Egyptian God Amon. An observer wrote: "The god neared his temple, illuminating heaven and earth with his beauty… His glowing rays struck the eyes of the people like a sunrise."

Offerings were made and other rituals begun when suddenly the ceremony was halted abruptly. In writings Thutmose III later described the incident:

"Amon began to move around on both sides of the hall of pillars and they who were before him did not understand what he was doing, when he was looking for me everywhere. Then he recognized me and stopped in front of me…I threw myself on the ground before him, but he raised me up and installed me in the king's place in the temple… The god himself placed me on the throne and I was adorned with the crown which was upon his head."

Although the priests carried the image of the god and had control of his actions, the people took the actions of the god as proof that the boy was chosen by him to rule over Egypt. No one dared question the action of the god fearing reprisal. And even Queen Hatshepsut was forced to stand by while this son of a harem woman ascended the throne.

For several years, Hatshepsut served as guardian of the boy, running the government in the boy's name. It soon became apparent that the queen was managing the affairs of the nation by reason of her own designs. The boy was easily bent to the will of his stepmother.

It wasn't many years afterwards when Hatshepsut convinced everyone that she should rule by herself reducing the title of Thutmose III to co-regent. It was no secret that the boy, now a teenager, was far from kind to his stepmother. He viewed with hatred the many monuments, statues, and buildings she had erected as a memorial to her rule. His day of vengeance would come.

Today there are no known monuments or records which tell of what actually happened to Hatshepsut. One day in 1483 BC she suddenly vanished from the face of Egypt. Thutmose III was suddenly the only ruler. One of his first actions was to demand the destruction of all of Hatshepsut's monuments. Her statues were torn down or defaced. Her inscriptions were ruthlessly hacked from walls and monuments. Hatshepsut's reign was treated by her successors on the throne as though it had never existed.

The nation was not in any great shape when Thutmose III took

Obelisk of Thutmose III relocated in front of the Lateran Palace in Rome Italy.

over full control of the government once again. Enemies were threatening on all sides. Now a strong military leader was needed for the very survival of Egypt.

The first test of Egypt's new military might was in 1457 BC. It was then that the Egyptian army led by Thutmose III went on to crush the great alliance of Syrian-Palestinian princes. For by doing so Egypt would head off any attempt at an invasion through Palestine.

Here in this decisive battle it was the military genius of the king, then just out of his teens, that insured victory for the Egyptians. The Egyptians had three choices of invasion from the south. The first was by a crook to the north that comes out on the plain north of the city. The second and easiest route curves to the east and comes out on the plain south of the city.

There was a third way, however, a way no officer in the Egyptian army would even consider. This was a narrow and arduous pathway through the mountains which led directly to the city.

In council with his generals, Thutmose III insisted that the last route, that of the narrow pathway, was the one to follow. The generals objected saying the route was far too dangerous and impassible. As a compromise Thutmose III said to his generals that he was going that way and if the generals wanted to go the easiest route they were free to do so. With that the army decided to follow their pharaoh.

In the end, it was by far the smartest move. The enemy, figuring the Egyptians would not invade by that route, had left it unprotected and the Egyptians gained entry without any problems. The city was left without any soldiers to defend it. When the Syrian and Palestinian army heard the city was under attack by the Egyptians they had to drop everything they had planned. They now had to head back to the city. But to defend it they somehow had to get inside the city's walls which were now closed.

It was an impossible task. As expected the Egyptians won it all in the end. With only a verbal promise that they would not again take up arms against the Egyptians, the enemy soldiers were released unharmed. They now could go as they pleased to their homes and families.

For Thutmose III it was a most successful beginning of a long line of successes

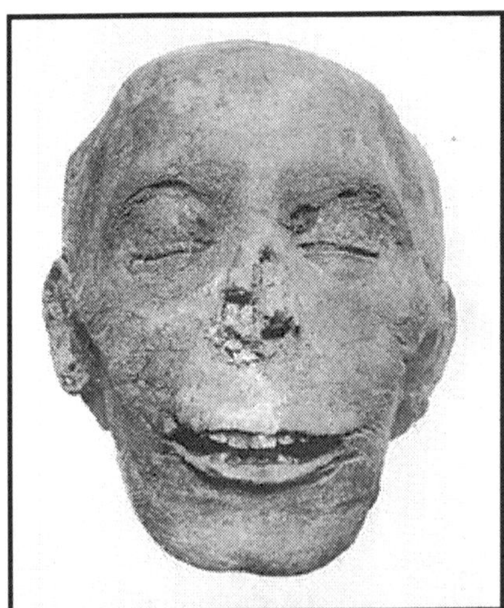

Mummy of Thutmose III on display at the Cairo Museum.

both in battle and at home. His name now was to be both feared and respected throughout most of the known world. Even today he is recognized as one of Egypt's greatest rulers.

Unlike many of the other greats in history, Thutmose III is not just another name on the rolls of history books. Those living today can actually see him face to face. For the mummy of Thutmose III can still be seen in the Egyptian Museum of Antiquities located in Cairo, Egypt. Seeing the remains of this man in person, visitors to the museum find it is hard to believe that Thutmose III's life came to an end some 3,500 years ago.

Tutankhamun (1341-1323 BC) His name became a household word

Wooden likeness of the young Tutankhamun on display in the Cairo Museum.

Tutankhamun was a boy of nine when he ascended to the throne of Egypt. He would reign for only ten years, dying suddenly at the age of eighteen. In those few years it was impossible for Tutankhamun to do a great deal for his country. He did, however, unify Egypt torn in religious turmoil. By recognizing and worshiping Amon as "king of the gods," Tutankhamun brought religious peace to his land. The pharaoh Akhenaton, who had preceded Tutankhamun, had sought religious reform and tried unsuccessfully to have his subjects worship only one god. However right this pharaoh was, his ideas came in the wrong place at the wrong time in world history. Egypt was just not ready for such thinking.

Tutankhamun's actions resulted in being highly praised by the priests and his people and by this one act, he would be remembered centuries later. For modern man, however, Tutankhamun was almost forgotten until the 1920s and 1930s when the name of Tutankhamun, now nicknamed King Tut, became a household word. For now, suddenly, King Tut was in the headlines of nearly every newspaper in the world.

The occasion was the discovery of King Tut's tomb complete with thousands of artifacts and treasures. No other time in history had such a discovery been made and not since that time have there been any other finds to match this one. For scientists and historians the event unraveled many of the secrets that for many centuries lay buried with the ancient Egyptians. For everyone, it seemed, it brought about a new awakening and interest in Egyptian history.

About Tut himself, science made some discoveries in examining the mummy. Among these was that he was slim in build and stood about five feet eleven inches tall. He had a slight cleft palate, and his spine leaned to one side making him walk to that side as well. He also had a partially clubbed foot. This made him unable to stand without some help. Most likely he walked with a cane. Several canes, in fact, were among the items in his tomb.

Shortly after ascending to the throne, one of the king's first acts was to marry his half-sister Ankhesenparton. At the time of the marriage the king was only twelve years old. His new wife was only nine years of age. In Egypt royalty marriages between brothers and sisters were common in order to keep descendant kings well within true royal blood lines. Early marriage was also accepted in ancient Egypt. In hot climates boys usually reach puberty by eleven and girls by ten.

From the beginning of his reign King Tut ruled all by himself. He was, however, very much influenced by temple priests and the military. He was pressed from all sides to reestablish the Egyptian empire to the glory it once was. Egypt at that time was shaken to its foundations by political turmoil. For the king it was a heavy burden to bear and especially difficult in that he was still only eleven and twelve years of age.

Nobody knows exactly how King Tut died or why. It is known that he died suddenly. When King Tut's tomb was excavated and his mummy examined it was discovered that on the king's left cheek were marks of a wound. Observers noted that this wound might have been the cause of his death. It was also determined that sometime late in his short life he had gotten malaria, which would have weakened his immune system. Close examinations also found a fracture in his left thighbone and a

Wooden bust of King Tut as a teenager on display in the Cairo Museum.

compound left leg fracture, which was obtained shortly before his death.

Putting all the evidence together, it was believed that King Tut was killed by an assassin. The reason was that there were objections by some to the king's actions in establishing the state religion in honor of the god Amon. It was also believed that it was because of the king's respect for the god Amon that other factions honored him as they did. And so they buried him in a lavish manner.

It took the Englishman, Howard Carter, five years to find the tomb of the king. These were five years of hard work, disappointments, and seemingly insurmountable problems. Then, after the discovery, it took another ten years to empty the

This golden throne used by King Tut was among the artifacts found in his tomb.

tomb. That was because of the magnitude of its contents. This long period was also due to the fact that the work could only be done in the winter months because of the extreme summer heat.

Carter also took his time to record exact locations of artifacts and direction in which they were placed. There was also the job of preserving, packing, and cataloging. There were many chests, sculptures, bow and arrows, clothing, gold lamps, furniture of all types, vessels of food, jewelry, and artistic works of all kinds.

In one corner were carriages and in another toys that the king used as a child. There were jugs, spears, shields, fans, gaming boards, musical instruments, and walking sticks. There was armor and some 300 weapons in addition to 278 arrows of all sizes. There were beds inlaid with gold and ebony, small tables and chairs from the king's nursery, models of ships, and four fine chariots, all with leather harness. In all there were some 3,500 treasures found in King Tut's tomb, a find unequaled before or after. All of the objects were handed over to the Cairo Museum where they remain today.

In his lifetime, King Tut did little to justify the fame that followed his death. His main accomplishment – that of reconciling himself with the god Amon, was done more so from a position of weakness than of strength. Yet by this one act, his name would live on the lips of Amon's followers for centuries to come. With all of this forgotten, he would again gain recognition in our own time, with the discovery of his tomb. Short as his life was, by an irony of fate, King Tut became in our time the most famous name in Egyptian history.

Alexander IV of Macedon (323-309 BC)
He was assassinated at the age of thirteen

In 342 BC, the last Egyptian pharaoh had been overthrown and Persian rule came to the ancient land of the Nile. But this rule by the Persians wasn't to last long. Just ten years later in the autumn of 332 BC, an army of Macedonians and Greeks, numbering some 40,000 men, invaded Egypt. Led by the young king of Macedonia, Alexander, later to be known as Alexander the Great, the invading army overran Egypt and overpowered the Persians virtually without a fight.

The Egyptians hailed Alexander as a liberator and later stood by in anticipation as Alexander was proclaimed king of Egypt. In order to appease the Egyptians he honored the numerous Egyptian gods. He conducted himself in contrast to the Persian conquerors that had outraged native feeling by renouncing the local religion.

He founded Alexandria, which was destined to become a world capital and one of the world's greatest cities. Then one day Alexander left Egypt to attack the Persian king in Mesopotamia. He was never to return. He died suddenly in Babylon in June of 323 BC.

It was Alexander's young

A portion of a painting of Alexander IV shown with his mother.

son, Alexander IV, who then took over the reins of government. He was just a baby born a few weeks after his father's death. Assisting him as joint king was Philip Arrhidaeus, a feeble-minded half-brother of Alexander's. Both ruled Egypt as well as other land holdings from Macedonia. The joint kings, in order to better rule the lands conquered by Alexander, appointed various Macedonian chiefs as governors of the various lands. It is assumed that he stayed behind in Macedonia. In Egypt the one appointed to rule was Ptolemy I.

Such an arrangement went on for six years when suddenly Alexander IV found himself the only king over the lands conquered by Alexander the Great. His uncle, and joint-king Philip Arrhidaeus, was murdered by the mother of Alexander the Great (Alexander IV's grandmother). At that time Alexander IV was only six years old and yet very much the ruler over the land. The Egyptians virtually worshiped the boy as the one chosen by the gods.

They raised giant statues of him and honored him in the temples. It was short-lived, however, for only seven years later Alexander IV, then only thirteen years of age, was murdered by Cassander, the ambitious governor of Macedonia. With the boy out of the way the governor proclaimed himself king of Macedonia. All of Alexander's other governors did likewise with Ptolemy I now king of Egypt.

GROWING UP IN ANCIENT EGYPT

Here's what young people had to contend with in ancient Egypt: It's a fact that one third of the children born in those years didn't live to see their first birthday. Out of those who lived, one half of these didn't survive past their fifth year. All of this was due to disease, accidents, and unsanitary conditions of the time. Children wore no clothes whatsoever until they were six years old. There were no schools, so they picked up only what their parents were able to tell them. They had few toys, just marbles, balls, and spinning tops for the most part. Due to the quality of food and other factors, lifespans for the lower classes were about 33 for boys, 29 for girls.

Ptolemy V Epiphanes (209-181 BC)
His twelfth birthday linked past and present

Ptolemy I and his descendants Ptolemy II, Ptolemy III, and Ptolemy IV ruled Egypt for the next 100 years. It was then that another boy ruler came to the throne of Egypt, Ptolemy V. He was only five years old and for the first time in many years the Egyptian government was paralyzed. Officials struggled for power and the common people seized the opportunity to revolt.

To prevent the boy's mother from being proclaimed guardian of her son, a successful plot was initiated with the result that she was murdered before she herself even knew of the death of the king. Agathocles and Sosibius, among those who plotted the murder, then manufactured a will that the late king was supposed to have signed. Reading it aloud to the people of Alexandria, with the new king at their side, the forged document proclaimed Agathocles and Sosibius the guardians for the young king. As guardians they would have complete authority over the government of Egypt.

Head sculpture of Ptolemy V.

The people of Egypt, however, did not accept the two guardians' story. They also had suspicions as to the events surrounding the death of the boy's mother. There were stories spreading through the streets of a possible murder. There was unrest in the military and threats all around Egypt's boarders of possible invasion. It was not the best of times for a new king, especially one as young as five years old, to take over the reins of government.

Vengeance against the two guardians and other court officials who helped plot the queen's murder was not far away. Troops under the command of Tlepolemus stormed the palace and seized the king. He was placed on a horse, taken to the stadium, and placed upon a throne in sight of the people.

A young officer then stepped up and asked the king whether he should deliver over the murderers of his mother to popular vengeance. The boy, dazed and frightened, gave the sign of assent. With this those responsible were dragged to the streets and lynched. Tlepolemus then became the king's guardian and regent. In a year he was replaced by another regent, Aristomenes, an officer in the king's bodyguard. When the boy king became twelve years of age, he ruled alone.

This coming of age in October 197 BC was a major event in Egypt. It was celebrated at Alexandria with great splendor. Later, in the old capital of Memphis, the young king was consecrated by Egyptian priests with the coronation ceremony due for a native pharaoh.

As it turned out the coronation had more far-reaching effects than the people involved ever dreamed. For the Egyptians it was just a routine proclamation they drew up in honor of his coming of age. This was incised in Greek and two forms of Egyptian on a piece of black basalt. That piece of basalt was found some 2,000 years later by modern archeologists. And it was that piece of basalt, named the Rosetta Stone, that served as the key to ancient Egyptian history. The ancient writings, lost for many years with nobody able to decipher them, were now understood. It became one of the most important historical discoveries ever made.

As for the occasion itself, the coming of age ceremony brought with it several acts of grace by the king for his subjects. Prisoners, including many who had been a long time in confinement, awaiting trial, were set free. Several taxes were abolished and others lightened. Certain debts owing to the royal treasury were remitted. Amnesty was granted many of

Egyptian coins minted during the reign of Ptolemy V.

those who rebelled against the government. And for the Egyptian priesthood, several new graces and concessions were granted as well as new honors paid to the national religion.

As a twelve-year-old, Ptolemy V was very active. Besides the acts of grace which eased many of the burdens of his people, he led an army which set out to crush rebel bands actively seeking the destruction of the present government. The rebels were tracked down by the king's troops to the town of Lycopolis, where the rebels had taken refuge. Taking the city by storm the king completely overpowered the rebels and crushed all of their resistance. Later, the leaders of the revolt were executed.

Four years later when Ptolemy V was sixteen years of age, he married a young girl by the name of Cleopatra. This Cleopatra, however, was not the one whose exploits with Julius Caesar are legend. That story would be more than 100 years and several kings away. This marriage of Ptolemy V, however, produced three children, two of them sons and one a girl, also named Cleopatra.

As a teenager, Ptolemy V was harsh-tempered and gained a reputation for cruelty and brutality. He had a passion for open-air sports such as hunting and athletic exercises. He was less interested in what the military was doing or in matters of state. Once, in an audience he had with foreign ambassadors the king fell sound asleep in his chair.

Had he lived longer, however, Ptolemy V would have led armies to recapture some of the lands lost by former rulers of Egypt. He often spoke about such conquests to his ministers. But Ptolemy never had that chance. His life came to an end very suddenly in 181 BC. Ptolemy V was just twenty eight years old. It is not known exactly how the king died or for what reason. It is believed he was poisoned.

Ptolemy VI Philometor (185-145 BC)
He was the most honest and virtuous
of Egyptian rulers

Headpiece of Ptomey VI.

When Ptolemy V died he left behind two young sons and a still younger daughter. The eldest, Ptolemy VI, was known as Philometor, or "lover of his mother." It was he who at the age of five then became king of Egypt as Ptolemy VI.

But Ptolemy VI did much more than just respect his mother, Cleopatra. He honored as well his brother and sister and strove throughout his life to keep peace in his family. He was probably the most honest, virtuous, and peace-loving pharaoh of Egypt that that land had ever known.

Part of Ptolemy VI's good nature probably came from his mother who set an example. She was by his side when he presided over state functions. She had no real ambitions and strove only to handle the affairs of the young king when he was still much too young to make major decisions. She maintained peace in the land and did not trespass on the rights of other kingdoms. In all things she maintained the alliance Egypt had with Rome.

She instructed her son in the right ways to live and the right path to govern. And when she died in 173 BC, Ptolemy VI, then only thirteen years of age, never let her down.

One of Ptolemy VI's first acts was to marry his sister. She was only twelve, her husband only fourteen when the marriage took place. The couple's brother, then thirteen years of age, would become king only if the two did not have children of their own. But unexpected events happened in Egypt that would make for a very unusual situation.

It all started at the death of Cleopatra (Ptolemy VI's mother) when two fire-eating ministers became highly influential in Ptolemy's court. They dreamed of making war with Syria and regaining that land lost to Egypt in previous battles. The new king at the head of the Seleucid Empire, which Syria was a part of at that time, had ideas of his own. That included war with both Rome and Egypt. And that is just what happened.

Both Roman and Egyptian soldiers lost in their efforts to hold back the movement of the Syrian forces. And so successful was the enemy here that the soldiers marched right to the gates of Alexandria. Ill advised to make an escape, Ptolemy VI was captured outside the gates. Rome in the meantime sent messages to the effect it would not stand by and let Egypt be conquered. Fearing a major reprisal against him, the Syrian king backed off. He did, however, keep the Egyptian king as his prisoner.

Fearing that Ptolemy would not return and that they would not have a leader, the Egyptians placed Ptolemy's brother on the throne of Egypt. This brother, then fifteen years of age, had the full rights and powers of a king.

Since the Syrian king could not conquer Egypt without seeing the whole of the Roman army come against him, he thought of a scheme, which in any other time might well have worked. He would set Ptolemy VI free to go back to Alexandria. With now two kings in Egypt he envisioned a major civil war. This alone could have caused the collapse of Egypt without an invasion from the outside.

The Egyptian kings and their sister Cleopatra foiled the scheme, however. Without a fight the two brothers agreed to rule Egypt jointly. Cleopatra would maintain her position as queen and wife of the eldest brother Ptolemy VI.

Visibly annoyed by all of this, the Syrian king marched into Egypt once again. His army stopped again at the walls of Alexandria, preparing to storm the city. But his plans were foiled once again. The gates of the city opened wide and one person, unarmed, walked out to meet the Syrian king. It was the Roman ambassador. Speaking in the powerful name of Rome, the ambassador ordered the king out of Egypt. Knowing full well that he could not win in any major confrontation with Rome, the Syrian king backed away. Without a fight he turned his army towards home.

For the next five years, the brothers continued to rule jointly. But the years were anything but peaceful. There was a great deal of strife within the royal family, Ptolemy VI continually trying to maintain peace and hold back his much more ambitious brother. While the brother was filling his mind with evil schemes and had engaged in all types of wickedness and cruelties, Ptolemy VI was beside himself, but always there with forgiveness and generosity.

Such admirable actions were completely out of character in those times of violence and cruelty. In those days, as for many centuries before and after, kings and kings-to-be thought nothing of killing off their brothers or sisters, fathers or mothers if it meant more power for them. Such action was taken in his own family – Ptolemy II and Ptolemy IV, both killing their brothers in their claim to the throne.

Ptolemy VI, however, was marked by his tenderness and humanity. He was kind and understanding of those who served him. And history records no single Alexandrine who suffered death by his will.

Statue of Cleopatra in the British Museum in London.

The Later Ptolemys (Cleopatra, Ptolemy XII, Ptolemy XIII, Ptolemy VIV) History was all around them

After the death of Ptolemy VI, it was about ninety-five years before another boy ruler would take the throne of Egypt. Ptolemy XII (117-51BC), who ruled from 51-47 BC, was the first. This was followed in rapid succession by Ptolemy XIII (62-47 BC), who ruled 47-44 BC and Ptolemy XIV (47-30 BC), who ruled 44-30 BC.

None of these made any real contribution to the kingdom of Egypt. All three, however, had two major things in common. All were involved in some way with one of the most fascinating stories of them all – the story of Caesar and Cleopatra. And all were killed – the first in battle, the other two only to keep them permanently out of the way.

Ptolemy XII was the brother of Cleopatra (69-30 BC), who co-reigned 51-30 BC. According to custom, was also

Cleopatra's husband. Ptolemy XII was only nine years old, Cleopatra, thirteen at the time of their marriage. Their father had left the kingdom jointly to the two when he died that same year in 52 BC.

From the very beginning, Ptolemy XII was only a puppet in the hands of his evil ministers, Achillas and Pothinus. Because they couldn't control Cleopatra, they fought to drive her from the throne and succeeded in doing just that in 47 BC. She was back a year later, this time at the head of an army.

Cleopatra's army met her brother's army at Pelusium. The battle, however, was never to take place. Julius Caesar, then the undisputed master of the Roman Empire, interceded. Reconciliation mended the fences between the two.

The peace, however, was short-lived. Another sister, Arsioneo, seized upon the general discord and declared herself queen. At war, protecting his throne once again, Ptolemy XII was drowned in a sea battle.

With Ptolemy XII now out of the way it was the custom that a younger brother, if one existed, would take over in his place. There was such a brother, then ten years old. He was immediately married to Cleopatra and reigned as Ptolemy XIII.

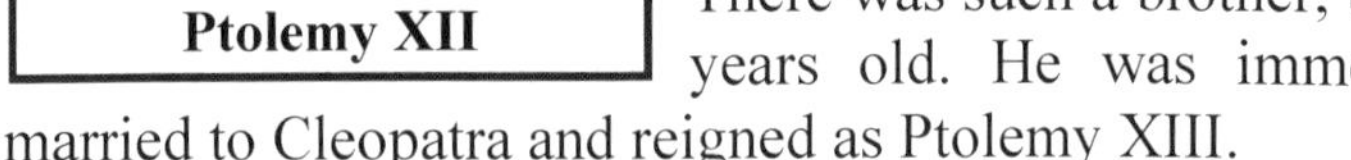

Ptolemy XII

It was at this time that the romance between Caesar and Cleopatra had flared which resulted, just a year later, in the birth of a son named Caesarion. It was he who would later become Ptolemy XIV.

The younger brother (and now husband) Ptolemy XIII, however, wasn't around long. With the scene dominated by Cleopatra, he had very little power. After Caesar's assassina-

tion in 44 BC, Ptolemy XIII demanded more of a say in the government. That was his first and
last mistake. Cleopatra promptly
had him executed. He was just
fourteen years old.

It was Caesarion's turn now –
the son of Caesar and Cleopatra.
He was then three years old. Lacking any more brothers, Cleopatra
placed him on the throne, jointly
with herself. She gave him the title Ptolomy XIV.

At this time Anthony came into
the picture. This was followed by

Ptolemy XIII

the birth of two more children, a boy and a girl. Several more
years had come and gone. Then, when Caesarion (Ptolemy
VIV) was seventeen years old, Cleopatra committed her well-
publicized suicide. Following custom Ptolemy XIV would
then marry his ten-year-old half-sister. But that was not to
happen. Declaring full control over Egypt, Octavian, then emperor of the Roman Empire, had Ptolemy XIV executed along
with a younger brother, least they serve as nuclei around
which revolts would form.

Octavian, however, didn't feel it necessary to execute a ten-
year-old girl. She would be married off in some far corner of
the world where she would never be a danger. This then ended the Ptolemaic dynasty and an era in Egypt.

CHINA TODAY

RUSSIA
KAZAKHSTAN
MONGOLIA
KYRGYSTAN
Urumqi
Shenyang
NORTH KOREA
Beijing
Dalian
Tianjin
Yinchuan
SOUTH KOREA
Qingdao
YELLOW SEA
CHINA
Xian
Shanghai
Chengdu
NEPAL
BHUTAN
Changsha
EAST CHINA SEA
INDIA
Guiyang
Guilin
Xiamen
CHINESE TAIPEI
BANGLADESH
Macau SAR
Hong Kong
MYANMAR
VIETNAM
THE PHILIPPINES
©World Guides
THAILAND
SOUTH CHINA SEA

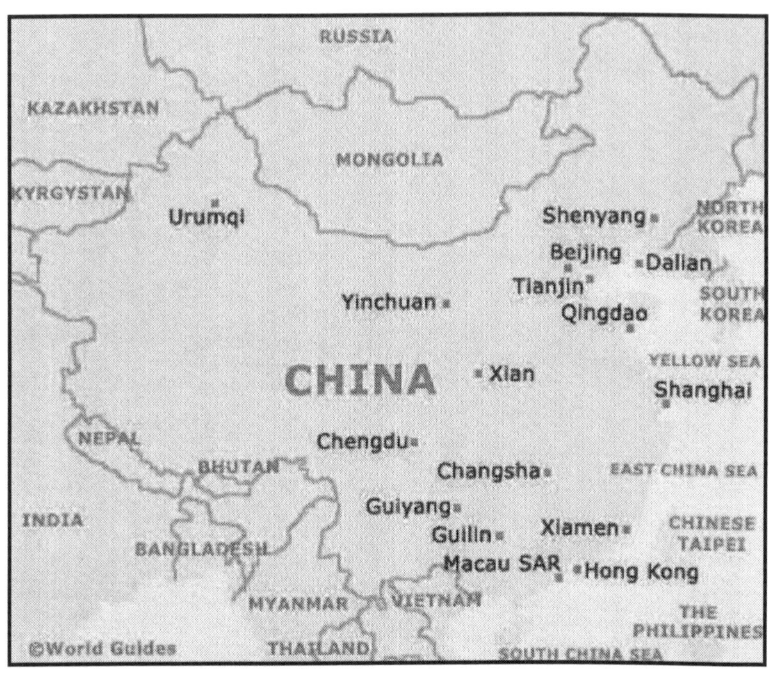

CHAPTER 2
CHINA

We never counted the number of rulers China has had over the centuries. We know there were a great many. What we do know is that among all of these, some of the most important, some of the ones who contributed most to their nation and the world, are among the child rulers listed here. And while many turned out to be ruthless and cruel men, they are still remembered for their many good deeds and accomplishments.

For the sake of organization, Genghis Khan, one of the greatest of world conquerors, is included with the stories of the Chinese emperors. His conquests began in Mongolia and included lands that are now China. Mongolia in turn was later part of China for a time and then part of Russia before it became independent in 1990.

There is one thing to note about these Chinese rulers. That is their names. Unlike most rulers in the world, the Chinese seemed to have several names. They were even given a new one when they became an emperor. It can be and often is confusing.

Qin Shi Huang (259-210 BC)
He was the father of his country but no role model

Of all of the rulers of China, without a doubt the meanest of them all was Qin Shi Huang (also known as Shih Huang Ti, Ying Zheng, and Zhao Zheng, among other names). He became emperor at the age of

Qin Shi Huang

thirteen. Through his orders about a million and a half people were killed, many in very cruel and lingering deaths. And yet, at the same time, he did more for his nation than anyone else had done up to that time.

One of his greatest accomplishments was the construction of the Great Wall. This wall stretches along the western border of China and is over a thousand miles long. It was built to keep the savage Mongol tribes from sweeping out of their deserts to attack the cities in China. It not only did that job well for several years, but because the project was so massive it became one of the Seven Wonders of the World, rivaling even the great pyramids in Egypt.

Besides all of that, Qin Shi Huang did something else, which makes him well remembered in China today. He brought his country together. What was once a smattering of independent states constantly warring against each other now became one united country for the first time. Qin Shi Huang also brought order to this new, united nation. In doing this he planned an entirely new system of government and for the first time China prospered.

For Qin Shi Huang all of this started in 246 BC. He was thirteen years old at the time and in his lap fell the responsibility of putting a nation together. As emperor one of his first orders was to have the arms collected of those who were not in his own forces. These arms were then melted into bells and huge statues. In addition he ordered the powerful and wealthy people in the country to move to the capital city. It was his idea that here they could be kept under surveillance in case any of them had any ideas of obtaining more power. This move also lent more dignity to the office of the emperor.

Once this was done, Qin Shi Huang rapidly became master of his own region. Then he set out to conquer everybody in sight. One observer remarked, "He ate up his neighbors as silkworms devour a leaf."

One campaign followed another in the years from 230 BC

A small portion of sculptures, found in recent years, depicts thousands of warriors that were to accompany the Qin Shi Emperor in death.

to 222 BC, until all the feudal states had been conquered, annexed, and brought under the emperor's rule. Through all of this, however, there were remarkable developments in civilization and a wide extension of Chinese culture. A new day had begun for Eastern Asia.

The cost of all of this was the absolute suppression of all those who dared criticize the emperor. Severe laws were drawn up and enforced. To do away with the old customs and ideas and inaugurate his own, the emperor found it necessary to have a book burning. He ordered that every historical book in the land should be collected and burned. Scholars who violated the command by hiding books in their homes were executed. To support the war and the extensive public work projects such as the Great Wall, Qin Shi Huang's taxed his people heavily. He was not a popular emperor.

Although Chinese historians have condemned Shih Huang Ti's many misdeeds, European scholars generally treat him as one of the greatest men in world history.

**A portion of the Great Wall of China
built by the Qin Shi Emperor.**

SPECIAL NOTE: For the next eleven centuries after the reign of Qin Shi Huang there were a string of child rulers. They reigned periodically from 200 BC to 1174. Some lasted several years, for others it was just days. Nevertheless, each had an impact in the history of China. Because this was ancient history, in most of these reigns little is known of their childhood years.

Emperor Zhao of Han (94-74 BC)
At last an era of peace

Emperor Zhao of Han reigned 87-74 BC. He became the leader of his country at age eight and reigned for thirteen years, dying at the age of twenty. During this time he lowered taxes and reduced government spending. The country as well enjoyed an era of peace. The exception was within the emperor's own family, most who continued in their quest for power.

Emperor He of Han (79-106)
He was kind and gentle

Emperor He of Han reigned 88-105. He ascended to the throne at the age of nine and stayed in power for nineteen years. He was described as kind and gentle. He was also humble and unassuming. He also appeared to genuinely care for the people, but lacked in the ability to govern or to judge character.

Emperor Shang of Han (105-106)
He was only 100 days old

Emperor Shang of Han reigned 105-106. He was placed on the throne when he was barely 100 days old and died a few months later, an infant the entire time.

Emperor An of Han (94-125)
He said now he didn't have to study

Emperor An of Han reigned 106-125. He was twelve years old when he took over the reins of government. Because he was in charge he said he reasoned that he didn't have to study, and didn't. He also had no interest in government. Instead, for the next nineteen years he indulged himself in women and heavy drinking, and paid little attention to what was happening around him.

Emperor Shun of Han (115-144)
People had great expectations for him

Emperor Shun of Han reigned 125-144. He was declared emperor at the age of ten. When this happened the people had great expectations that things would improve. His father, after all, was considered not only incompetent, but violent in his actions. His son's biggest asset was that he was kind. Because of this it allowed the people a measure of peace. But the emperor trusted others who should not have been trusted, causing some pain. Even so, living conditions improved. Shun died at the age of thirty after reigning for twenty years.

Emperor Zhi of Han (138-146)
His remark didn't go well

Emperor Zhi of Han reigned 145-146. In most cases, being remarkably intelligent and wise is a good thing. It didn't do well for Emperor Zhi of Han, who came to power in China at the age of seven. Immediately the young ruler recognized trouble in a powerful general named Liang Ji. He recognized the fact that this general had great influence in the government and wasn't doing it well. When the seven-year-old emperor remarked in public his dislike of the high-ranking official, it didn't go over well. The remark was overheard by the general, who within a short time managed to poison to death the young emperor. He was just eight years old at the time and had served only a few months on the throne.

Emperor Chong of Han (143-145)
He was just two years old when he died

Emperor Chong of Han reigned 144-145. Emperor Chong of Han was just one year old at the time he ascended to the throne in China. He was the son on Emperor Shun of Han and his concubine consort Yu. During his reign, his father's official wife, Empress Dowager Liang, and her brother, Liang Ji, presided over all government affairs. Yet, while she was open minded and honest, her brother was not. As a result this led to corruption, which put great hardships on the people. The emperor, due to his age, was unable to act. Then, to complicate things further, the young ruler took ill and died. At the time he was less than three years old.

Emperor Ling of Han (156-189)
Everyone helped themselves
to the state treasury

Emperor Ling of Han reigned 168-189. He was chosen to be the new emperor when he was about twelve years of age. He reigned for about twenty-one years until his death in 189. At that time, he was about thirty-three years old. During his entire reign the government was infested with a great deal of corruption, everyone taking what they could from the state treasury, all the while vying for more power. This was particularly the case of the eunuchs who were assigned to the palace. Unfortunately, the emperor not only looked the other way but did nothing when it was observed right before his eyes. The emperor, in fact, was part of the problem. As he grew older he preferred to indulge in women and a decadent life-style rather than take care of government affairs. He sold po-litical offices for money and seldom would listen to those who came to him to point out problems in the government. This resulted in several rebellions and a further weakening of the government.

Emperor Shao of Han (176-190)
He served for just five months

Emperor Shao of Han reigned 189-190. He became emperor at the age of thirteen, but before he could get anything done he was poisoned to death. He served his country just five months. Doing the deathly deed was the warlord Dong Huo, who at the time had full control of the country. None in the capital city dared oppose him.

Emperor Xian of Han (191-234)
He had to escape from his own palace

Emperor Xian of Han reigned 189-220. He was the younger half-brother of his predecessor, Emperor Shao. The warlord Dong Huo put Xian in place after killing his brother. At the age of eight there was little the new ruler could do but go along with everything he was told. Later, two other warlords assassinated Dong Huo and they in turn took control of the government. It wasn't until six years later that the emperor was able to escape the city where he soon became stranded.

A year later another warlord, Cao Cao, rescued him before overthrowing the other two warlords. But rather than putting the emperor back in power, he kept control himself. When Cao Cao died in 220, his son and successor Cao Pi forced Emperor Xian to abdicate. But rather than put Emperor Xian to death, he was allowed preferential treatment and lived peacefully for the rest of his life.

Emperor Cheng of Jin (321-342)
He survived rebellions, battles, and relatives

Emperor Cheng of Jin reigned 326-342. Emperor Cheng was just four years old when he was proclaimed emperor. Because of his young age, the administration was dominated by a string of regents. Two of his uncles were among them. But despite rebellions among the people and various battles, the emperor remained on the throne, gradually gaining the full reins of government. When he married, both he and his new wife were fifteen years old. Just six years later, Emperor Cheng became gravely ill and died. He left two young sons still in their cradles.

Emperor Mu of Jin (343-361)
His first act: to get married at age 13

Emperor Mu of Jin reigned 347-361. He was just one year old when he came to power, but as an infant he knew nothing of what was happening around him. Mu, however, learned quickly, and by the time he was thirteen years old, he was in complete control of the government. His first act was to get married. He reasoned that the rest of his duties could wait. Five years later, Emperor Mu was dead of unknown causes. He was still a teenager at age eighteen.

Emperor Xianwen of Northern Wei (454-476)
He was the first emperor to voluntarily retire

Emperor Xianwen of Northern Wei reigned 465-476. He was just eleven years old when he became emperor, and there was hope that he would become a great leader, making life better for his people. Instead of devising ways to make life for others more miserable, he was devoted to studying various philosophies and religions. Those who knew him said he was also honest in his dealings and hardworking. However, instead of putting all this to work in governing his country, he decided to give it all up in order to spend more time in his studies. He ended up being the first emperor in Chinese history to voluntarily retire. He turned power over to his four-year-old son, and for the next eleven years he lived as he wanted. It wasn't as long as he may have wanted as he died young, at the age of twenty-two.

Emperor Xiaowen of Northern Wei (467-499)
He wanted his country united in all things

Emperor Xiaowen of Northern Wei reigned 471-499. Officially he became emperor at age four because his father, Emperor Xianwen, got tired of ruling and wanted more time for other pursuits. His father remained in place, however, to help his young son in those early years. Unlike his father, the new ruler wasn't as interested in those other pursuits as he was in making changes in his country. These changes could be reduced to one word—unity. He forced everyone to speak one language, to wear similar clothes, and be united in all things—all to reflect one Chinese culture over others. Emperor Xiaowen had only a few years to see change. While he outlived his father, he died young as well, at age thirty-two.

Emperor Ziaoming of Northern Wei (510-528)
He enjoyed those romps in the imperial gardens

Emperor Ziaoming of Northern Wei reigned 515-528. Due to disease and the lack of medical knowledge, those who lived in ancient times didn't live long. The lives of rulers through-

out the world were often even shorter. This was not to disease, but to murder by members of their own household. Such
was the case of Emperor Ziaoming. He became emperor at
age five. From the very beginning he enjoyed spending most
of his time in the imperial gardens. Even as he grew up he
didn't seem to be that interested in learning about important
affairs of state. In Emperor Ziaoming's case, this wasn't a
problem. Because when he reached the age of eighteen and
before he could do much in the way of ruling, he was poisoned to death by his own mother.

Emperor Jing of Northern Zhou (573-581)
This new ruler was killed by his own grandfather

Emperor Jing of Northern Zhou reigned 579-581. He became
emperor at the age of six after his father, Emperor Zuan, for-
mally passed the throne to him. His father, however, continued to help his young son for another year before he died. The
new emperor's maternal grandfather, Yang Jian, seized power
at this point and forced the emperor to yield power to him. He
then had the seven-year-old emperor killed, along with several
members of the household who the grandfather considered a
threat.

Emperor Gong of Sui (605-619)
The emperor never had a chance

Emperor Gong of Sui reigned 617-618. Amid battles among
warlords, one of them, Li Yuan, made the thirteen-year-old
Gong the new emperor. Then, less than six months later, the
same warlord forced him to officially turn control of the government over to him. To seal the deal, the general quickly
killed off Emperor Gong. At no time in his short life did Emperor Gong have any influence in the government.

Emperor Xizong of Tang (862-888)
He survived the turmoil on all sides

Emperor Xizong of Tang reigned 873-888. When Emperor Xizong took over the government of China in 873 he was eleven years old. From the very beginning the country was in turmoil and a major drought had impoverished a great portion of China. Warlords fought one against another, each controlling sections of the land. As a result, the emperor himself was forced to listen to the military leaders' demands. Nevertheless, the young emperor survived the turmoil for the next fifteen years. A serious illness caused his death in 888. He was twenty-six years old.

Emperor Ai of Tang (892-908)
There was little hope for this new emperor

Emperor Ai of Tang reigned 904-907. Warlords in China continued to dominate at the time Emperor Ai began his reign. The new emperor was just eleven years old and his father had just been assassinated. There was little hope Emperor Ai would succeed in such an environment. He didn't. Within three years he was forced to abdicate. Not long after, he as well met his end, poisoned at the hands of the warlord Zhu Quanzhong.

Emperor Guo Zongxun (953-973)
This six-year-old was deposed, sent away

Emperor Guo Zongxun reigned 959-960. Emperor Guo Zongxun was just six years old when he became the ruler of China. Within the year he found himself deposed by General Zhao Kuangyin, who founded the Song Dynasty. The now former emperor was then sent away with his mother with the assurance that they would be treated with respect. That was the case for a few years, but it didn't last. Xin Wenyue, an official trying to gain favor with the new emperor, killed Guo Zongxun. He was just twenty years old.

Emperor Renzong of Song (1010-1063)
This emperor encouraged his people in cultural pursuits

Emperor Renzong of Song reigned 1022-1063. Emperor Renzong was twelve years old when he became the ruler of his country. He was said to be merciful, tolerant, and modest. He was also watchful on just how he spent the government's money. The emperor also encouraged cultural pursuits among the people with a particular emphasis on reading and writing.

Unlike previous rulers, he was against using the death penalty unless absolutely necessary. He

Emperor Renzong

was particularly concerned that someone would be put to death for a crime who later would be proved to be totally innocent.

Despite all of this, rebellions were numerous, mostly due to high taxes that kept many in a state of perpetual poverty. Worse, in 1048 a great plague hit China hard causing many deaths.

Emperor Zhezong of Song (1076-1100)
Emperor and country suffered from a bad grandmother

Emperor Zhezong

Emperor Zhezong of Song reigned 1085-1100. He took over the government when he was just nine years old, but the real power was in his grandmother, who acted as regent. Only when she died and the emperor was seventeen, did he take complete control. His father, the previous emperor, put in place several reforms which improved the lives of the people. The grandmother, however, revoked all of those reforms. Only after she died did Emperor Zhezong re-establish them. The reforms included the lowering of taxes, low-interest government loans to peasants, and a gift of horses to help peasant families in need.

A well equipped Chinese warrior defending the homeland against invading forces.

Genghis Khan
(1162-1227)
He was the world's
greatest warrior

Genghis Khan

Though not an official emperor of China, there are few, if any, scholars anywhere in the world who don't regard Genghis Khan as one of the greatest warrior rulers of all time. He started the Mongol conquest of China that was then completed by his descendants. As important as he is, however, seldom do they talk much about his childhood. In reality, however, it was these early years that set the stage for the kind of ruler he was yet to become.

It all started when Genghis Khan was only thirteen years old when he became chief of his tribe. Because other chieftains were out to conquer him it was a matter of survival to fight back. He went beyond that, however, and not only maintained his freedom, but with the help of his armies conquered not only other tribes, but invaded China, Korea, Persia, and Russia. At his death, his kingdom stretched from the Pacific to the Volga River and from Siberia to the Persian Gulf.

When he was very young, he fished, tended herds of horses, and rode on his horse into open areas in search of lost animals. He had the job of seeking out new pasture lands and watching for raiders. There were many hardships such as sleeping in the snow without a fire and going for days at a time without food.

For fun, he enjoyed racing horses twenty miles out into the prairie and back. He became a marksman with the bow and arrow. But most of all he enjoyed wrestling. In this activity, breaking a bone here and there was nothing unusual. The eight-, nine-, and ten-year-old Genghis Khan was not all that admirable. Besides seriously hurting a friend in a wrestling match he had virtually no mercy for his friend or anyone else. Once when one of his half-brothers stole a fish from him he never asked any questions. He, without even thinking about it, merely killed his brother.

He had just barely turned thirteen when he went riding out with his father. Far from home, the two were invited to spend the night in the tent of a strange warrior. The young boy immediately set his eyes on the warrior's daughter. She was just nine years old. After looking at her for some time he asked his father if he could have the girl as his wife. Despite both of their ages, a marriage between the two was arranged. The decision made, it was agreed that Genghis Khan would remain at the girl's house to get to know her better. The boy's father, in the meantime, left the tent of his new friend to handle tribal business.

A few days later a messenger arrived with word that the boy's father lay dying, the result of poisoning. The messenger said the chief had asked to see his son. When the boy arrived, however, his father was already dead.

It was custom among the Mongol chiefs that the leadership of the tribe fell on the chief's oldest son. Expecting this, nearly two-thirds of the leading men had already deserted the tribe before the boy had arrived at his father's bedside. The men were afraid to trust themselves and their families and herds to an inexperienced boy.

So, now with just a small band around him, Genghis Khan knew what might happen. And that was that all of his father's foes would most likely take advantage of the situation and attack without mercy. At his father's death, however, knowing the uncertainties that lay before him, he did not flee. Alone, he sat beside his dead father and wept. There was his mother to take care of and his sisters and younger brothers to feed. And there were those of the tribe that remained – expecting the leadership that would protect them from invaders.

There was no time, however, to ponder the situation. Before he could leave the tent of his dead father an invasion had already begun. The first duty of the invaders was to kill Genghis Khan and claim leadership for them. Genghis Khan, his brothers, and his sisters had no recourse then but to flee. The invaders, it was believed, would seek them, and at least for a time, leave the rest of the tribe alone.

This proved true. The invaders had nothing on their minds except the death of Genghis Khan. The hunt began, but the hunters made no great haste. The trail was fresh and clear, and the nomads were accustomed to track down a horse for days if need be. Eventually, they figured, they would close in on him. Genghis Khan didn't make that an easy task.

The new chieftain and his family headed for the shelter of gorges with timber growth to screen them. To make the task more

Genghis Khan shown on a modern day Mongolian banknote.

difficult for their pursuers they stopped long enough to chop down trees covering the narrow trail. Later they separated, Genghis Khan's brothers and sisters finding shelter in a cave while Genghis Khan himself broke a trail away from the area in the hope his pursuers would follow him and not find his brothers and sisters.

He rode toward a tall mountain range and once there concealed himself for several days. But the enemy did not give up. They waited. Hunger and thirst forced the boy to risk capture. So, late at night he tried quietly to sneak through the enemy lines. It didn't work. The boy was spotted and captured. A wooden yoke was put over the boy's head which, when secure, rested on his shoulders. At both ends were holes that held his wrists. Thus he was led away to the enemy camp.

For a while it seemed as if all was lost. The boy worried about his brothers and sisters. He was concerned about the members of the tribe that remained loyal to him. Now, with his capture, all could be lost. But the chain of circumstances which followed, even Genghis Kahn would not have believed possible.

It all started when the boy found himself late at night alone in a tent with only one guard. All was quiet. It was time now, he thought, to attempt an escape. So he snuck up on his guard and whacked him in the head with his wooden yoke. With the guard now knocked out, the boy crept through the camp, plunged into the brush, and made his way to the river nearby. He discovered that he didn't have much of a head start. The enemy was in quick pursuit. The boy knew he couldn't outrun them so, when reaching the river, he entered the water, sinking down among the rushes near the bank. Only his head was above water. Here he would wait, hopefully until the men gave up their search.

Again his plan didn't have much success. While several men searched the riverbank, one of the men spotted him. But as luck would have it, instead of reporting the find or lunging at the boy with his spear, the man said nothing. The man urged the others to abandon their search in that particular area and he and the others left to return to camp. Genghis Kahn was again by himself.

It was then that he did a very strange thing. Instead of continuing his journey he returned to the camp of his enemy, found the tent of the man who had saved his life, and asked

Mongolian warriors in battle with the Chinese.

his help. The immediate need was the removal of the wooden yoke about his head which prevented him from defending himself or obtaining food or water. It turned out that the man was not a regular member of the enemy camp but a traveler who had only sought temporary food and lodging. He agreed to help.

The man split the wooden yoke, removed it, and burned all of the evidence in his fire. He then hid the boy in his cart, which was loaded with wool. He later brought the boy food and a bow with two arrows. Then, the man packed up his other belongings and with his cart in tow, went on his way. Once out of sight, however, he stopped and the boy made his escape.

When Genghis Khan finally made his way back to his own camp, he found only the ashes from the fires. His herds were gone, his mother and brothers vanished. Still not giving up, he was on the road once again, this time following the trail of his family. An accomplished tracker, the task was not all that difficult; so it wasn't long before he caught up with them.

What he found was his family in hiding, hungry and afraid. So, leaving them alone once again, he hunted game, brought it back, and prepared a meal. Then he prepared them once again for more running. They traveled by night, made their way through enemy lines when need be, and sought aid along the way from friends. The boy was more cautious now. From that time on, no person ever made Genghis Khan a prisoner again.

As the young man traveled with his family, it happened that eight of the nine horses, which the family owned, were stolen in the night. The ninth horse was spared only because Belgutai, one of Khan's brothers, was away on a hunting trip. When

**Fifteenth century artwork showing
Genghis Khan traveling with three of his sons.**

the brother returned, Genghis Kahn informed him of the stolen horses. He then boarded his brother's horse and went after the thieves. The crime was a serious one in those days because it put the entire family except one on foot. All would be at the mercy of any raiders who might come along.

Even though the horse in which the boy rode was tired, Genghis Khan quickly picked up the trail of the thieves. But as the thieves were able to change from one horse to the other, they kept well ahead and out of his sight.

For several days, the chase continued until one day Genghis Kahn spotted another young boy milking a mare beside the trail. Explaining what had happened, Genghis Kahn asked the boy if he had seen the horses and any men driving them.

"Yes," the boy said. "Before dawn eight driven horses went past me. I will show thee the trail they took. My name is Borchu and I will ride with thee after the horses."

Without asking, Borchu took from Genghis Kahn his tired old horse and put it out to graze. He then roped and saddled a white horse from the heard he was tending and offered it to his new friend.

It was three days before the boys came upon the raiders' camp. The eight horses were grazing nearby. Observing the men for some time, the boys then rode after the horses, rounded them up, and drove them away from the camp. This roused the men and one of them mounted a white stallion and gave chase.

Without stopping or hesitating any more than to glance over their shoulders at the approaching man, and his friends not much further behind, the boys drove the horses faster and faster toward their home. But as nighttime approached they noticed the approaching rider was getting much too close. So Borchu dropped back, strung an arrow, took aim, and let go the string, striking the man in the chest. He fell to the ground and the others approaching from behind gathered about him.

The boys didn't wait around to see what their followers would do next. They continued in their flight with their string of horses. They drove the horses on through the night until at last they came to the camp of Borchu's father.

Explaining his absence, Borchu told his father their exploits. "When I saw him weary and anxious," Borchu explained, "I went with him."

The father was understanding and congratulated the two on their bravery. "Ye are young," he said. "But ye are now friends and continue to be faithful."

After a rest in Borchu's camp, Genghis Kahn was given food and a gift of black fur for his family. Genghis Kahn was grateful. He spoke to his new friend, "Without thee I could not have found and brought back these horses, so half of the eight are thine."

But to this Borchu would not agree. "If I should take what is thine from thee, how could thou call me a friend?"

After this time, the reputation of Genghis Kahn grew among the many tribes. His clan increased rapidly. Many of those who had followed his father had returned. Others admired his skill in evading his enemies and holding onto all the important pasture lands, and joined as well. Cunning kept Genghis Kahn alive and a growing wisdom assured him that he would be master of his heritage.

All of this had a great influence on the troops. They felt proud of the spirit and energy which their young prince displayed. They were more and more resolved to exert themselves to the utmost in defending his cause.

Genghis Kahn was just thirteen years old when probably his most important battle was waged. A great army, whose leaders challenged his right to lead the Mongols, had gathered near the camp of the young prince. It was a challenge that had to be met with force. So Genghis Kahn gathered his troops about him and with the help of experienced generals, planned the battle.

When all was in readiness, Genghis Kahn took his place at the head of his troops and went forth to attack the rebels. The rebels were ready to receive them – thirty thousand strong, according to historians. Horsemen filled the open plain and charged one another at full speed. Showers of arrows filled the air, many finding their targets. Then, because they were too close to use their bows and arrows, the men discarded them and drew their sabers. Outcries of agony and triumph were equally mingled on the battlefield. Through it all, the boy ruler fought courageously right along with the others. In the end the battle was won and the enemy put to flight.

Genghis Kahn managed to pass through the battle without being hurt. Having fought with such energy and purpose in the field, he was not any longer considered a boy. He was immediately recognized by all the army as their sovereign and fully entitled to rule.

Genghis Kahn in turn accepted his powers with calmness. He made addresses to his officers and soldiers and distributed honors and rewards to them. With the battle won, nearly the whole country occupied by the rebels submitted without any further resistance. Other tribes, who lived on the borders of his dominions, sent in representatives with treaties of alliance. Genghis Kahn was well on his way into the pages of history.

Genghis Khan mausoleum located in Ejin Horo Qi, Inner Mongolia.

A military genius, he soon became Khan of all the Mongols. He invaded China, Korea, Persia, and Russia. He was, in fact, one of the most renowned conquerors whose exploits history records. At his death, his kingdom stretched from the Pacific Ocean to the Volga River and from Siberia to the Persian Gulf.

SPECIAL NOTE: After the conquests of Genghis Khan, there were several more child rulers of lands of what is now China. For the following seven rulers, little is known of their childhood years on the throne.

Emperor Gong of Song (1271-1323)
This five-year-old had to surrender

Emperor Gong of Song Dynasty reigned 1275-1276. Emperor Gong was just four years old when he was made the leader of his country. It was a time when China had been invaded by the Mongols. As a result, within the year the then five-year-old boy was forced to surrender. Remarkably, he wasn't killed but allowed to live peacefully. Forty-seven years later, however, the emperor at that time didn't like one of former Emperor Gong's poems. As a result, he was forced to commit suicide.

Emperor Duanzong

Emperor Duanzong (1269-1278)
He was constantly on the run from invaders

Emperor Duanzong reigned 1276-1278. For seven-year-old Zhao Shi, who was to be the new emperor of China, there was no peace. He was constantly on the run from an invading army. His younger brother, the Emperor Gong, had already surrendered to the Mongols, and Zhao Shi, his other brother, and several ministers managed to escape to Fujian Provenance, where a new capital was being established.

Here, Zhao Shi was enthroned as the new Emperor Duanzong.

It mattered little as the Mongols managed to break through the Chinese lines. And again the newly crowned emperor and his brother and others were on the run, this time to Hong Kong. It was near here that the young emperor fell off a boat and almost drowned. After this he became ill and died a few months later. He was just nine years old.

Emperor Bing

Emperor Bing of Song (1272-1279) With a final naval battle lost, so went the country

Emperor Bing of Song reigned 1278-1279. At Emperor Duanzong's death, the crown went to the remaining brother, who now would become six-year-old Emperor Bing of Song. At the time, there was little hope things in China would improve.

Nevertheless, a large naval battle ensued in a last effort to save the country from the Mongols. The result was that the entire fleet was wiped out by the enemy. Now, as all was lost, Lu Xiufu carried the now seven-year-old emperor to a nearby cliff. Here they committed suicide by throwing themselves into the sea. The emperor led what was left of his country for just 313 days.

Ragibagh Khan (1320-1328)
A case of bad timing for this new emperor

Ragibagh Khan reigned 1328-1328. He was briefly installed as the ruler of China at the age of eight. It was bad timing. At the same time, a Mongolian commander had launched a coup, a civil war broke out, and the emperor's army was defeated. As a result the leading loyalists were taken prisoner and executed, including the eight-year-old emperor. He ruled only a few days in 1328.

Rinchinbal Khan (1326-1332)
He was emperor for just three weeks

Rinchinbal Khan reigned 1332-1332. He was just six years old when he was placed in charge, ruling as emperor of China for just three weeks in 1332. He died of unknown causes, never reaching his seventh birthday.

Toghon Temur (1320-1370)
He was one of the few child emperors
to experience a normal lifespan

Toghon Temur reigned 1333-1370. Also known as Emperor Huizong, he became one of the few rulers of China who started out as a child and lived to enjoy a somewhat normal lifespan. Becoming emperor at the age of thirteen, he held onto control until he was forty-nine years old. At that point he was overthrown in the Red Turban Rebellion. This marked the end of Mongolian rule in China and the beginning of the Ming Dynasty. His time in power, however, was not easy. He dealt not only with droughts, floods, and famine, but rebellions and revolts of all kinds.

Emperor Yingzong of Ming (1427-1464)
This eight year old reigned fourteen years

Emperor Yingzong of Ming reigned 1435-1449. Very little is known of this emperor's early life and rule. What we do know is that he became the emperor at the age of eight and ruled for fourteen years until he reached the age of twenty-two. He lived, however, for another fifteen years, dying at the age of thirty-seven.

GROWING UP IN ANCIENT CHINA

If families had the means in ancient China their male children were sent away to school. Here they attended classes all day long, seven days a week, concentrating on reading and writing. For the vast majority of children, however, there were no schools for them. These children learned what they could from their parents and spent most of their time in the fields planting rice and feeding the chickens.

They ate using chopsticks and had their meals at dawn, midday, and sunset. In their spare time they played with toys such as marbles and kites, and engaged in games such as hide-and-seek, an activity that was popular throughout the world.

If a kid misbehaved they weren't punished as they were in most other countries, but were told ghost stories to scare them. Families were most important and several generations lived together in one house, sharing responsibilities.

Despite a lack of opportunities for many young people, ancient China was a land of invention, being the first to introduce paper and printing to the world. At the time, China was also way ahead of most countries in science and technology, math, and astronomy.

Wanli Emperor (1563-1620) An empire obtained, then thrown away

Wanli Emperor

After the rule of Emperor Yingzong in 1449, it was 124 years before another boy ruler came to power in China. His name was Wanli who also went by Shen T-Sung. Born in 1563, he became emperor of all of China in 1573 when he was but ten years old.

From the very beginning, however, Wanli never really had a chance. He was very much under the influence of his tutor, the senior grand secretary Zhang Juzeng (AKA Chang Chu-chan). The court was torn by factions. Ministers who did much of the work for the emperor were not well liked. There was a lot of corruption and misgovernment. Taxes were oppressive. There was rebellion among the people. Those who favored the minister's way of handling things were given large estates and power over the people. Those who opposed the ministers were often executed.

Wanli, given bad advice and direction, was doomed to be a failure as an emperor. More often than not he was incompetent. Yet not without some redeeming social value, he sometimes acted with decision and dignity.

With all the problems at home, the Chinese people were ripe for an invasion from outside. And that is just what happened. First it was the Mongols. Then in 1592 the Japanese invaded Korea. Korea, as a Chinese vassal, appealed for Chinese aid. At first the Chinese army had no success. But in 1598 the Japanese were forced to abandon Korea. Instead of going home, however, the Japanese then invaded China, often massacring whole towns and burning down the looted houses. During Wanli's reign, China was also waging war in Annam, Burma, and Siam. Later, the Manchus began to attack the Chinese cities in Manchuria. Then, by 1618 the Manchus conquered the greater part of Manchuria.

Wanli Emperor 1572 coin.

Conditions in the capital itself worsened with virtually everyone with any amount of authority struggling for power over others in the court. And it was many years following the death of Wanli in 1620 before matters were settled in China.

The Soul Tower of Emperor Wanli.

Shunzhi Emperor

Shunzhi Emperor (1638-1661)
He gave up his throne

Nearly a half dozen emperors ruled China between Wan-li and the reign of Shih-Tsu. (also known as Shun-chih and Fu-Lin, and later Shunzhi Emperor). He was just six years old when he was crowned emperor in 1644. Unlike many of his predecessors, Shunzhi was a youth of an affectionate and loving disposition. He willingly submitted himself to the guidance of Kau-Kumg and Chang-Chu (ministers to his father) to whom he had been entrusted.

Although Shih-Tsu, who was now proclaimed Shunzhi Emperor, performed many of the duties of a ruler, even at his young age, he did not perform them all until he was twelve years old. The high spirits which had marked his childhood, however, had already given way to the seriousness of his high office. One of his first edicts was that he laid out regulations for controlling entrance to the priesthood. Public education also interested him and he was active in the revision of the system of examinations for degrees.

The personal character of the emperor was exceptional for his time. There were no scandals or intrigues in his court. The emperor himself and those who worked in his behalf were respectable servants of the people.

By modern standards, however, the emperor's character changed somewhat when he became fifteen years of age. It was then that he married the Impress Tung Chia. At the same time, however, he acquired a concubine, his favorite being the Lady Tung. It was this Lady Tung, not his legal wife, who spent the most time with the emperor and her death virtually altered the course of Chinese history.

The emperor loved her very much, partly because of her beauty, but mostly due to her personality and disposition. She was accustomed to admonish the whole court on festive occasions to spare the drink, to dine wisely and not too well. She worked very hard to keep the emperor up to the mark in his public and private life. She would reprimand him if he skimmed over the fine print in legal documents, insisting he read every word. And she gave of herself, attending personally to the comfort of the emperor.

The emperor was deeply in love with her. It was a shock to everyone that she died so young in the autumn of 1661. No one missed her more than the emperor. For her death affected Shunzhi with uncontrollable grief, from which

In ancient China concubines were often favored but never replaced the empress.

he never recovered. So much was his grief that he voluntarily handed over the government to four of his ministers, stepped down from the throne, and left the crown to his youthful son, K'ang Hsi.

A writer during those times wrote: "He threw away the Empire as one who casts away a worn-out shoe; he rejected the sovereignty thrust upon him in this incarnation, and, following the example of the Lord Buddha, preferred to seek the mystic solitudes."

Shunzhi Emperor's decision to reject his way of life certainly was prompted by the death of Lady Tung. It had long, however, been his ambition to become a monk as expressed in the following words he wrote as a teen-ager:

> "The future is as dark to me as the past out of which I have come; vainly have I lived through one existence in this world of men. I have yearned to become a devoted follower of the Lord Buddha; Why, then, do I still hanker after the vanities of the Imperial Throne?"

At the time of his abdication, Shunzhi was only twenty-three years old. He had become emperor at the age of six and had ruled his nation for seventeen years. It was his wish now to conceal his identity from the people of China, his whereabouts only known to his son K'ang Hsi and his ministers in the capital city.

His first acts were to disguise himself as a commoner and mingle in the crowd in order to witness the ceremonial procession of the new emperor, his son. Having done this he became an abbot of the T'ien T'ai Temple, which lies amongst the hills, fourteen miles to the west of Peking. Officially he was declared dead and the common people of China never heard from him again.

Kangxi Emperor (1654-1722)
He was probably China's greatest Ruler

Kangxi Emperor

Historians, comparing the great rulers of the world, have declared K'ang Hsi of China (also known as Xuanye and finally Kangxi Emperor) as being among the best. In personal ability he was said to be probably superior to such rulers as Peter the Great of Russia, Louis XIV of France, and William III of England. He expanded his nation, adding Formosa, Siam, and part of India to his realm. He made sure his land was governed by personal visits. He pretty much founded education in China, encouraging it to the point that China was printing more books than anywhere else in the world.

He developed a friendship with the west, believing that by learning their ways better understandings could be maintained. He had the will and ability to lead and dominate men. He was actively concerned with the welfare of his subjects and was very conservative in his own and the court's expenses. He fostered not only material prosperity but also cultural activity. And through it all he gave to China as vigorous an administration as the empire had ever known.

One might wonder if a vision of Kangxi Emperor's greatness might have been experienced by his father Shunzhi. And even though Kangxi Emperor was only seven years old at the time of his being proclaimed the ruler of his country, one could only imagine the thoughts of Shunzhi as he watched the ceremony from amongst the crowd. Certainly he must have known he was leaving the empire in good hands.

As the father had respect for his son, so did the new emperor have respect for his father. For the young emperor often visited his father at the T'ien T'ai Temple. When, in 1670, his father died, Kangxi Emperor had a life-sized statue of him cast in bronze. He also sent yellow dragon robes for which to clothe his father in death and presents of pearls and jewels to be buried with him in his tomb.

Though he was very young, Kangxi Emperor insisted on doing only what was right and just. But he was very much hampered in doing this because of the Board of Regents appointed by his father to help him administer the government. Those regents incurred his displeasure by their harsh treatment of the Roman Catholic fathers. He was also angered by the imprisonment of Adam Schaal, who had been appointed his special tutor. It wasn't until the young ruler became thirteen years old, however, that he was able to dismiss the regents and assume full control of the government.

From that time on, he ruled the empire wisely and strongly. He attended to his duties with a great deal of purpose and direction. At sunrise every day he met with his advisors and dealt with every problem that arose, from laws and taxation to armies and foreign wars. He took it upon himself to visit even the furthest provinces to see that the government was treating the people fairly. Wherever he went he talked freely and pleasantly with both rich and poor.

He was described as having large bright eyes that lit up his face that was pitted with smallpox. Fairly tall, he was said to be well-proportioned and attractive. He also was said to have engaging manners, was truthful, clever, and fond of study. His love for books began when he was only five years old. Later, by his orders, scholars set to work compiling encyclopedias and a dictionary in 1,628 volumes. This love for learning led him to make friends with Christian missionaries who came to China. It was by this exchange of ideas that made him so well known in western lands. In all things he was known as an honest and fair ruler.

He enjoyed hunting and devoted three months of every year to this pursuit. While still a teenager he was out riding on one of these hunting expeditions when he came upon an old farmer sitting by the side of the road. The man was weeping loudly.

"What is causing you so much sorrow?" asked the emperor who was dressed in a rough hunting coat and therefore not recognized.

"All my life I have lived on the little farm that my ancestors left me," the farmer said. "I have worked hard to provide what little food we have. But the mandarin of this district liked my land and took it from me and took my son to

Kangxi Emperor on Tour.

be his servant. I am left homeless and alone."

The emperor dismounted. "Get on my horse, good grandfather," he said. "You and I will go to this mandarin and make him give back your land."

The farmer realized then that this person was someone of importance and refused, out of courtesy, to mount the horse and leave the young lad without transportation. The emperor then took the farmer up behind his saddle and together they road to where the farmer said the mandarin lived.

Realizing at once the youth was the emperor, the mandarin knelt on the ground. The emperor had no mercy. He ordered the mandarin's arrest and presented both the farm and the son back to the farmer.

Such an occurrence was very unusual in China in those days. Both earlier and later emperors often never ventured beyond the palace gates. They also allowed mandarins and other officials to do anything they pleased. Not so with Kang-xi. He demanded both excellence and obedience among those who served him.

As skillful as he was with governmental matters, he was also a master when it came to the military. When he was still in his teens, he faced a possible overthrow of his government by several military leaders. They had rebelled because of the control the emperor was placing on them. They felt they, not the emperor, should have the say in military matters.

For a while things looked very bad in China. Many Chinese joined in the uprising. There were battles in many areas. Soon more than half of the area of China proper was in the hands of the emperor's foes. So much was their success that the rebels had already raised up one of their number as their new leader. It seemed that all was lost.

Boy ruler or not, he was going to show them who was their leader. In the days to follow he showed himself fully equal to the emergency. He directed his loyal armies at every front. He took advantage of dissensions among the ranks of his opponents. It didn't happen overnight, but slowly his troops began to regain the lost territories. In the end he was victorious and his rule was even more firmly established than ever before.

Kangxi was great in the eyes of the world as well because of his character, his wise government, his deep learning, and his prowess in both war and domestic affairs. Probably his most prominent quality was his kindness of heart. This, coupled with the policy that China's ruler must be firm, made him one of the most important rulers of all time. When he died in 1722 he was sixty-eight years old. For China it had been more than sixty years of Kangxi's rule. They were good years, years the country would long remember.

Tongzhi Emperor
(1856-1875)
Meet China's juvenile delinquent

Tongzhi Emperor

There is little recorded of the life of Tongzhi (also known as Zaichun) who became emperor of China in 1862 when he was just six years old. Part of the problem was that Tongzhi lived only until he was eighteen years old. He served in the capacity of emperor for just twelve years. As ruler, he was given a new name, Tongzhi Emperor. The first part of his reign was devoted to inner-fighting among court officials as to who should run the country and how. The last half of his reign was not devoted so much on the workings of the nation as it was on the private life of the emperor himself.

Tongzhi by far enjoyed the wild life of Peking in which he spent most of his time, to the heavy duties of being emperor. Even as a young boy he was running the streets getting into all kinds of mischief. His escapades on the town became the scandal of all of Peking. He was a frequent visitor to the city's theatres and brothels. He was mixed up in drunken and disreputable brawls and would often return to the palace long after daylight and the hour fixed for audiences with foreign dignitaries.

When he wasn't on the town at night he was out on the town in the daytime. It was then he would visit the book and picture shops where he could purchase lewd carvings and paintings. All of this was with the express approval and often encouragement of those assigned to look after him. The feeling was that with the emperor out of the way they could do as they wished in running the government.

There were times, however, when the emperor was sober and took time out for the occasions of state. One of these obligations was the duty of receiving foreign ambassadors. One of the problems in this, however, was the question of etiquette. A great deal of correspondence between Chinese and foreign ministers was undertaken on the question of whether an ambassador was required to kneel in the presence of the emperor. To make things easier Tongzhi decided the he would accept three low bows in lieu of the kneeling procedure.

When the emperor was fourteen years of age, he was brought into one of the rooms in the palace. There in front of him were two young girls, one of which he was told would be his wife. It was the custom in those days that a suitable wife would be picked for the emperor and the marriage arranged before the emperor even saw his future bride. In this case, however, court officials were undecided which of these two girls would be the best wife, one faction choosing one and another faction choosing the other.

It was mutually decided that to decide once and for all, the emperor must make the choice himself. So when presented with the two, the emperor quickly chose A-Lu-Te. It so happened, however, that A-Lu-Te was not the choice of the emperor's mother. She in turn scolded the emperor long afterwards for his "bad" choice. And, still hoping to rectify things, she tried to force the other girl on the emperor every chance she got. It didn't work. Instead of accepting his mother's offer he spent more and more time out on the town.

It was from one of these episodes that the emperor caught the disease that finally did him in. As he lay on his death bed the eyes of A-Lu-Te became swollen with weeping. His death was a sore blow to his unhappy widow now pregnant with his first child.

It was A-Lu-Te's own father who feared problems by A-Lu-Te's pregnancy. Feeling vengeance would be wreaked on his family by others in their play for power, A-Lu-Te's father thought it best if she committed suicide. It cannot be imagined that she did this voluntarily. Nevertheless, two hours after the death of the emperor, A-Lu-Te also was dead. Certainly the life and death of the emperor Tongzhi was not one of the better chapters in Chinese history.

Long after his death, however, the emperor's city escapades were still the talk of all of China. To give more credence to the stories, visitors would often be shown the small opening just outside the palace gate where the emperor made his exits and entrances. As the main palace gates were closed in the evening, the emperor had this special opening just for him.

**Eastern Qing Tombs located in Zunhua, China
is the burial place of Tongzhi Emperor.**

Guangxu Emperor

Guangxu Emperor (1871-1908) This ruler lacked leadership and lost a war.

Upon the death of Tongzhi Emperor, a three-year-old, the emperor's cousin, Zaitan, was chosen as the new emperor. His reign name became Guangxu Emperor or Kuang-Hsu, which meant "continuation of splendor." For him and his kingdom it was anything but splendor during the thirty -three years that he led his country. The problems at first were similar to other rulers who, in infancy, suddenly found themselves with a crown on their head. While the boy ruler was still too young to know what was going on around him, those in authority positions in court fought one another. Each in turn sought more power for themselves.

When the young emperor started to participate, he was always too ready to accept the advice of his ministers. He was docile and he lacked in all the qualities of leadership. Moreover, he really never expressed any interest in statecraft, preferring to leave all the heavy decision-making to others.

In 1894, the Sino-Japanese War broke out over Korea. With Korea a protectorate of China at that time, China had to act and act quickly. There was little prepared even though Japan had long threatened war there. Despite the efforts of the Chinese armies, the war was lost. The terms of the treaty were that China was to relinquish her protectorate over Korea and give up Formosa.

China had problems with Russia as well. After several confrontations ending in 1858, China ceded certain territories in northern Manchuria to Russia. Later, Japan and Russia fought one another for the lands that China gave up. Japan won and Manchuria then went to Japan. It wasn't until the end of World War II that Manchuria was returned to China.

In the years of the Guangxu Emperor China was lagging far behind the rest of the world. It was evident that major reforms were needed. With the advice of others, massive reforms were placed into effect throughout the land. The reforms, however necessary, were enacted all too fast. China just wasn't ready. The result of this was that many patriotic Chinese were convinced that the empire was on the threshold of final disaster. There was a great deal of opposition in all sections of China.

The empress Tzu His, who had been part of the regency during the emperor's infancy, came to the front again. With her followers' help she ordered the arrest of all reformers in the government. The emperor as well was made a prisoner in a palace near Peking. And there he remained until his death in 1908.

Guangxu Emperor probably would have made a better ruler had he first not became a leader of his country so early in life. For those about him had established a good foothold in the government by the time he realized what his position was. He also didn't have the training such was given other rulers around the world. There was no real preparation for the job he had to do because those about him wanted to have control as long as possible. When that control was finally granted it was too late.

His one major accomplishment of initiating reform in his country probably would have succeeded. That was only if he had handled it more wisely, easing his nation into reform in gradual, cautious steps. As it was, even in this admirable area, he was doomed to failure. In the end he had accomplished nothing.

Puyi
(1906-1967)
It all ended here with this last of China's boy emperors

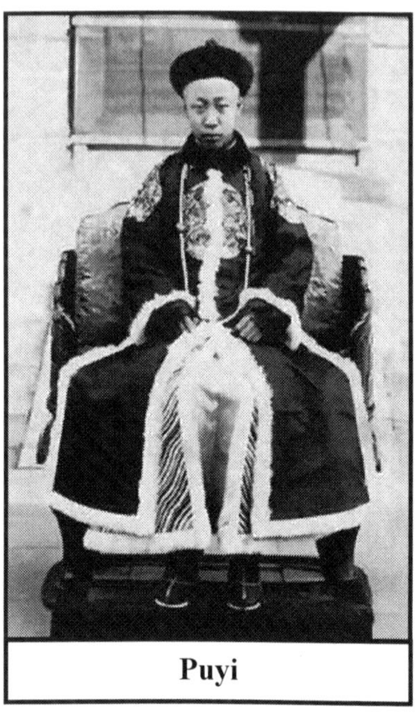

Puyi

Born in 1906, Puyi was just two years old, two months shy of being three, when he became emperor of China. It all started when palace officials and a group of eunuch attendants arrived at his family residence. With little warning and no time to take anything that belonged to him, he was picked up and forcibly taken away.

The small boy screamed, not knowing what was happening to him, not being familiar with those around him, not knowing where he was going or why he was leaving. He didn't know it at the time, but he would never see his home or be in those familiar surroundings ever again. Even his mother was kept away. It would be seven years before she was allowed to visit. By that time the young boy, then eleven years old, would have only a vague memory of her.

If being forced from his home on that day wasn't bad enough, a short time later he was to face one more uncomfortable situation – his coronation. Still a toddler and still not knowing what was happening, it was for him overwhelming. Even though he was carried onto the throne by his father, the scene before him was frightening. Here, in a large and strange facility known as the Hall of Supreme Harmony, it seemed to be everything but harmony. There were throngs of people. There were deafening vibrations of ceremonial drums beating, sound from varied other musical instruments, voices talking, even shouting all around him. As a result he started crying. His father, whispering in his ear, "Don't cry, it'll be over soon," had little effect.

Even after this ordeal was over, there was little his father could do to calm him down. It took a nurse to get him under control. In the years to follow he became very fond of this nurse. But then, another jolt: as he turned eight years old, on that day she was taken away from him.

From the very beginning the emperor, now living in the Forbidden City, was never given the opportunity to have toys or to play and behave as did other children of his age. None of the adults around him were allowed to discipline him. He was free to do as he wished in most things.

Later in life, the emperor wrote about these early experiences. "Those around me were strangers. They were remote and distant," he wrote. "Everywhere I went, grown men would kneel down, averting their eyes until I passed. In the palace I was never without eunuchs around me. They waited on me when I ate, dressed, and slept; they accompanied me on my walks and to my lessons; they told me stories. They never left my presence and were my earliest teachers."

But any good relationships they had were short-lived. The emperor overheard conversations among the eunuchs that made him fear for his life. As a result he had all of them evicted from the palace, never to return.

Replacing them was a Scottish academic and diplomat, Reginald Johnston. He served as Puyi's tutor and advisor for five years. Puyi was thirteen years old when he arrived. And, with the guidance of Johnston, he learned western ways. He was also introduced to an array of information that included geography, history, and science.

In the midst of this, however, when Puyi reached fifteen years of age, court advisors thought it was time for him to be married. As with tradition they brought Puyi four photographs of young girls. He was to choose one of these for his wife.

A portion of the Forbidden City.

There was no option on meeting them and getting to know them in person. Puyi said later all of the photographs looked alike and chose one at random and then another as his second choice. His handlers, however, didn't agree with his first pick and selected for him his second choice, a girl named Wanrong.

Hundreds were invited to the ceremony. But rather than respecting the occasion, many of the invitees decided to loot the palace. Puyi, writing about the party afterwards, said it was total chaos. "The pearls and jade in the empress's crown had been stolen. Locks were broken and areas ransacked," he wrote. By the end of the day a fire broke out that destroyed a section of the palace. The emperor said later that he suspected it to be an act of arson, just to cover up some of the thefts.

Being so young in the earlier years, it was impossible for the emperor to rule the country by himself. So from the very beginning of his reign a group of individuals were assigned to help the emperor in overseeing the country's business. The regency appointed, however, was weak. As a result, the unrest in the country at that time was not adequately handled. The protests turned into open revolution. Rebels organized taking into their control one province after another. The leadership tried on several occasions to make peace by granting concessions of every kind.

It was too late. Completely overpowering the emperor's armies, the rebels declared the nation a republic and even went as far as to naming a president and forming a parliament. In total defeat, Puyi was forced to read the following edict:

"The dynasty has been carried on for near
-ly 300 years. I, your descendant Puyi,
since my enthronement, have endeavored
to consummate the constitutional program,
but my policy and my choices of officials
have not been wise, hence the recent troubles. Fearing the fall of the sacred dynasty,
I accept the advice of the National Assembly and swear to uphold the nineteen constitutional articles and to organize a parliament, excluding nobles from administra-
tive posts. I and my descendants will ad-
here to it forever."

The agreement stated that the emperor would retain his title for life, receive a large income, and was to keep his private property and the use of a palace. This never happened. It wasn't long before Puyi was expelled from the Forbidden City. At this time the now former ruler was eighteen years old.

For China it was not a good time. Japan was expanding its empire and lands throughout the western Pacific were being overtaken. In 1932, China lost its area known as Manchuria as part of that expansion. Japan thought who better to govern that as puppet head of the government than one out-of-work emperor – Puyi. Already rejected by his native country, Puyi couldn't refuse.

The Japanese re-organized the land as the state of Manchukuo. Puyi was chosen to become "Chief Executive" of the new state. Here he ruled as a figurehead until the end of the war, Japan surrendering in 1945. Manchuria was then returned to China and Puyi was imprisoned for ten years as a war criminal.

The great nation of China, however, was not at all through with its problems. There were yet to be more struggles and even more changes in the government. One thing was fairly certain, however. The monarchial institution in China, which had its beginnings in prehistoric times, would be no more.

ENGLAND TODAY

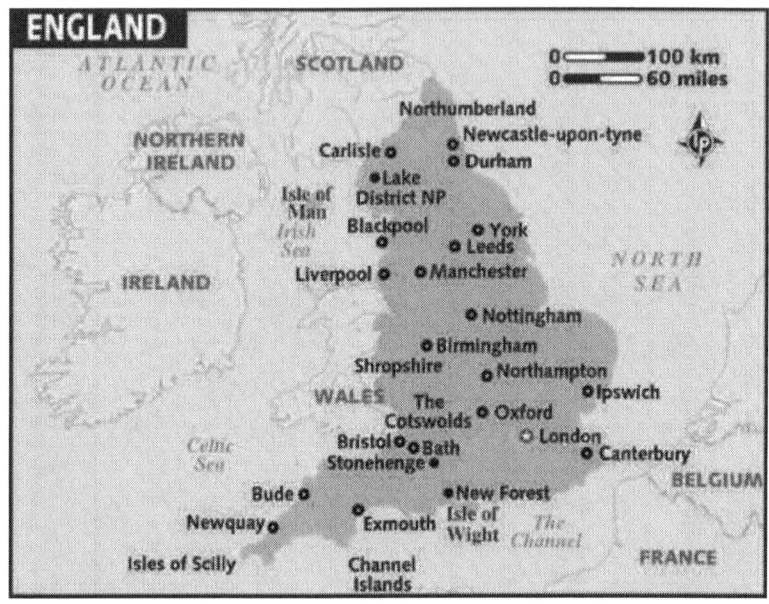

CHAPTER 3
ENGLAND

There is a faintly remembered legend in England about an ancient king in the days when the country was split into four small kingdoms. When this king died he left his throne to his saintly eight-year-old son, Kenelm. The boy, however, had an older sister who didn't feel her brother should have gotten the crown. She wanted it for herself.

So, she conspired with others. Plans were drawn up and executed with the result that the small boy was murdered and his body buried in a pass in the Cotswolds. The sister was then queen and her first order was that anyone who as much as whispered the name of Kenelm would be put to death. It was her plan that with such an order, Kenelm would soon be forgotten.

It wasn't long after that, however, that a small, white dove circled in the air above St. Peter's Cathedral in Rome. When the bird saw the front door open it flew into the massive structure and headed straight for the alter. It was immediately noticed. After the bird's capture the priests discovered a piece of parchment which the bird carried in its bill. The papal scribes were called in, but nobody could decipher the language. Finally, an Englishman stepped forward and read the message. It told of the murder of the young king, the queen's part in the conspiracy, and even where the boy was buried in the Clent Hills.

A search was made of the area with the result that the king's body was found and the queen's part in the murder exposed.

Today, in the exact spot where the boy's body was found there stands a chapel, built to commemorate the event. It is in ruins and probably in time will disappear altogether. But even then, Englishmen will probably be talking about the boy king, his wicked sister, and a small white dove.

In modern England, however, there were but five boy kings – Henry III, Richard II, Henry VI, Edward V, and Edward VI. In their lifetimes are many stories of heroism, of good deeds and bad, of love and adventure, sorrow and death.

Henry III (1207-1272)
Someone had to be nice and Henry III was just that

Henry III was eight years old when they placed the crown of England on his head. The year was 1216. Henry may have been ready for the job before him, but the country wasn't. In the first place the crown jewels had been lost in the wash and there wasn't even a crown to place on the young boy's head. Hastily court officials searched for a substitute. What they found was a plain gold circlet. This was used in the coronation ceremony. Then, when it came to the coronation dinner, so ill prepared were the officials that even that had to be plain and hasty.

Henry III

There was very little happiness in the land. The treasury was empty. The French army had landed on the shores of England and had taken possession of London and most of the eastern counties. With all of these problems there was still another: the king was dead and the country was now in the hands of an eight-year-old boy.

The barons who filled the church for the new king's coronation must have had many uneasy feelings. It was no different with the common people in the streets. All, however, had enough of all the problems. And they wanted nothing now, save to see the French troops swept into the sea. The one who just might do that was the boy now before them – Henry III.

The crowning was done in the ancient Roman city of Gloucester. And, into the old church which good Abbot Serlo had built, crowded the small group of bishops and earls. At any other time the assembly would have held all the great men of the kingdom in their finest robes and glittering jewels. But the country was deeply involved in a war with France. There was neither time nor money to do the job properly.

Nevertheless, the streets were filled with people, the curious, straining their necks for a glimpse of the little king, listening for the boy's high-pitched voice as he would repeat the words of the oath. They wondered: What kind of a man would he grow up to be and what manner of monarch would he make?

From the very beginning his position was exceedingly weak. He could never say "no" to anybody. The nation was nearly bankrupt and on the verge of collapse by foreign invasion. But from some points of view his father's early death benefited his cause. Henry had no personal enemies and having fortunately no uncles, he had the prospect of growing up in no danger of being murdered.

His looks, however, didn't help. Chief among this was the fact he had a drooping left eyelid which covered half of his eye. As a result, this rendered him a rather sinister appearance.

Despite this, the more chivalrous of the barons gathered around him. And under the experienced regency of William the Marshal, Henry's affairs prospered beyond expectation. In time even the French invaders were expelled from the country. Yet, while Henry was still in his early teens, he was very critical of what was done for him. He was as determined as his father had been to prevent any restraints on his right to rule as he saw fit.

Yet, as he gradually did get those rights, in diplomatic and military affairs he proved to be arrogant yet cowardly, ambitious but at the same time impractical. Even though as a youngster he was kind natured, charitable, and cultured, he was still very young and lacked the ability to rule effectively. This never changed as he went through his teen years and young adulthood.

Westminster Abby, burial place of Henry III.

When he became older, he combated his poverty by ruthless, extortionate taxation. He suppressed the Jews in his country by extracting from them large sums of money. This crippled their ability to do business. He engaged in costly, fruitless wars. Due to all of this there were many civil disturbances and much dissatisfaction.

And yet, as odd as it may seem, from the time he was very young and through the years to follow, Henry was a likeable fellow. He was kind natured, known for his piety, holding religious ceremonies and giving generously to charities.

He did everything possible for his relatives and poor in-laws. He remodeled most all of the English cathedrals and rebuilt Westminster Abbey. He allowed Franciscan and Dominican friars to set up establishments in England giving impetus to works of charity. Finally, among the most noble deeds of all, he threw his palaces open to the poor, inviting them to come in and be fed. He may not have been a very good king, but in many ways, he was a very nice one.

Richard II
(1367-1400)
His courage was unmatched among kings

After the death of Henry III, a little over 100 years went by before another boy king took the throne. His name was Richard II and he took upon himself full control of the kingdom when he was just eleven years old. No one was appointed regent. Richard, according to parliament,

Richard II

was fully competent to govern himself. He was allowed his own great seal, privy seal, and signet, and the government transacted business in his name. He was as fully responsible for the activities of government as all the previous rulers of England had been.

He was born January 6, 1367. According to various sources, three kings – the King of Castille, the King of Navarre and the King of Portugal – were present at his birth. Just a few years later on July 16, 1377, at the age of ten, Richard was crowned king. Although he did have advisors and several others working in his behalf, from the very beginning he had great informal influence over the business of government. When others like counselors and friends did get to be too influential, increasing taxation and undertaking unsuccessful military expeditions, all it did was to earn the mistrust of the people. As a result the king's core of advisors and their significance was scaled back.

Richard's first real life-and-death test with his new responsibilities, and probably his finest hour, came about when he was just fourteen years old. At that time, in the summer of 1281, he was described as tall, good looking, and intelligent. This, and whatever other assets he had then, helped on that day when there erupted one of the most dramatic and significant events in English history – the rebellion of the peasants.

The problem came about because of certain land laws that kept a large number of peasants in utter poverty. Peasants were allowed to cultivate some acres of land belonging to the lord of a manor. In lieu of rent the peasants gave a portion of their time to the land reserved to the lord.

This, in itself, was not a concern with most peasants. But what became a major problem was the added right of the owner to call on them for extra work anytime they saw fit and without remuneration. Often this extra work came about when the workers' own crops needed harvesting and as a result were ruined. An added burden was the rule that the peasants were bound to the land and could never leave it without his lord's consent. His children were bound also even to the point that they couldn't marry without the approval of the landlord.

On top of all of this, Parliament had decided to levy a poll tax to pay for the war with France. This added tax was imposed on everyone over the age of fifteen. Already on the verge of starvation, the peasants refused to be taxed further. The only course of action was to revolt. And under the direction of a man named Wat Tyler, revolt they did. There were riots in nearly every section of England. The rebels even swarmed across London Bridge into London itself, murdering and looting everyone and everything in sight.

During the turmoil, King Richard, who had just entered his teen years, fled with his advisors to the Tower of London. The Tower was the safest place in London, the strongest fortification in all of England. There the king looked out over the city and saw it in flames. Nobody in the king's court, it seemed, could do anything to halt the violence. Without hesitating, Richard took a bold step. He decided to face the mobs.

A portion of the Tower Of London showing the turrets.

Appearing in one of the turrets of the Tower, he called down to those below asking them to go peacefully to their homes. Refusing that, Richard immediately made them an offer. He would leave the Tower and meet with their leaders the next morning. This could have meant his life and he knew it. Richard was determined to save his country. And it was only he at this point who even had that opportunity.

Richard kept his word. In the morning, accompanied by the mayor of London and a handful of lords and knights, he traveled by barge to the appointed spot. The weather was warm and the sun was climbing in a cloudless sky.

Thousands of rebels lined the riverbank. Some cheers were raised for the gaily dressed king, but most of the voices were clamoring loudly for the heads of his unpopular ministers. Seeing that the mob was completely lacking in order and discipline, the boatmen brought the barges to a standstill some distance from the shore.

The young king stepped forward and looked out over the mobs. As the noise eased he spoke. "Sirs," he said, "I have come to listen. What want ye?"

Almost in unison, the men demanded that the king come ashore. The leaders of the mob if they were there were not seen or heard. And the noise from the rebels was so loud that the king could not make himself be heard again.

Believing it a fatal mistake to put the king in the middle of such a mob, it was unanimously decided to turn the barges around and head home as fast as they could. Within easy shooting distance from the shore, the lords knew that the mobs had only to train their bows and arrows on the barges and all, including the king, would be killed. The rebels, however, did not raise a hand against the king. It was clear to everyone there that the peasants were sincere in their devotion to the king.

Richard's first effort to calm the peasants had failed. The rebels, still unsatisfied with things as they were, continued their rampages. It was evident that the king had to make the next move. After another uneasy night in the Tower, he agreed to a second meeting with the rebels. This time it would be on land and would be face to face with Wat Tyler himself.

At seven o'clock the next morning, Richard and a small chosen company rode out from the Tower. Immediately peasants swarmed about the royal party yelling out their demands for changes in the laws and punishment of the head ministers who had ill-treated the common people for so long. So many rebels were there along the way that Richard's horses were slowed to a walk. And so loudly were the cries that Richard's two older half-brothers dropped out of line and road swiftly back to safety.

Richard, however, did not yield. He was smartly dressed in a coat of blue and silver and he rode steadily onward. Once at the appointed meeting place he stopped and met Wat Tyler and his officers. He never left his saddle. As Tyler read out the peasant demands, Richard listened. He asked questions. He smiled. When it was over Richard agreed to the rebel demands that the land laws would be changed, that landlords would no longer have dominion over them.

Instead, the peasants would have the status of tenants and pay so much per acre to the landlord for use of the land for farming. The rebels also demanded that a complete amnesty be extended to all participants in this uprising. This, also, Richard agreed to do. What wasn't agreed to, and Richard was very firm in his stand, was the request that the king's ministers be punished for extended wrongdoings toward the peasants.

"There shall be due punishments," he said, "for those who can be proven traitors by due process of law." Richard said he would go no further than that.

Most of the peasants accepted those terms and soon were on their way home, carrying the news of their new freedoms. Many of the peasants, however, were either not happy or had not yet had their fill of the murder and looting in the streets of London. Others still wanted revenge on the king's ministers. They felt it was now or never.

Richard returned to his castle and was in despair even more. If such civil disobedience was allowed to continue, what was to come of his kingdom? Richard decided he must try one more time. This time it would either be a lasting settlement or he would pay with his own life.

Preparing for the worst, Richard spent some time with his confessor and received absolution. Those who were to travel with him also filed through the chapel and they too made peace with their God. It was the feeling of many that they just might not return. The future of England was at stake, however, and all were willing to make that sacrifice, including the young king.

Then, the time had come. Two hundred men mounted their horses and King Richard led the small army toward the rebel camp. At a wide plain in front of the walls of St. Bartholomew the king's party stopped. There across the plain were several thousand rebels all drawn up in some pretense of military order.

A silence settled over the field. Finally the figures on horseback detached themselves from the rebel ranks. It was Wat Tyler and a banner bearer. When Tyler arrived within speaking distance of the king, Richard asked why the peasants had not returned to their homes. "All that you have asked has been conceded," he said.

Tyler answered by saying there was yet much to be discussed. He went on to list innumerable problems besetting the country at that time. It was clear to everyone that he was demanding the impossible. Richard, however, was not unduly moved by the demands. "Such changes would require much thought and earnest discussion," he said. "I will grant all that I have the right to concede saving the realities of my crown."

With this, Tyler turned his mount ready to return to his troops. But before he went on his way a voice from the ranks behind the king spoke up. "I recognize this fellow. He's a notorious highwayman and robber."

The remark inflamed Tyler. He kicked the flank of his mount and rode head on into the ranks about the king. He drew his knife and slashed out. In defense the king's men

Artist rendering of Richard II shown at a feast.

drew their swords and Tyler was wounded. He turned his horse away and was heading back to his men when he lost his balance and fell, crashing to the ground. Tyler was near dead.

Seeing all of this, the rebels left their ranks and charged frantically toward the king's men yelling, "Kill! Kill!"

It was then that Richard rose to the occasion with true courage. Not waiting for anyone to follow him, he sped his horse forward, out to meet the rebels single-handedly. "What need ye, my masters?" he yelled. "Ye seek a leader? I am your captain and your king. Follow me."

Utterly surprised by the unexpected move of the king, the rebels stopped in their tracks. They stared in wonder at this youth who faced them alone. They forgot about their leader who lay dying near their feet. They thought only of their king. They turned and returned to their previous positions, the king riding with them. They began to ask him questions. Was he to keep the promises he made? Would he work with the common people? Would he try to make life better in England?

Meanwhile, the king's men saw their king disappear into the ranks of the rebels. Was he safe? Would he be killed or held as hostage? They were overwhelmed in numbers. There was no way any of them could survive an attack. They made no move. Realizing the situation could be critical, one man rode back to London at top speed. He sent criers about the streets, alerting the people that the king was in the hands of the rebels.

The response was instantaneous. From all sections of the city young and old brought what weapons they had and gathered about the messenger. There was and estimated army of some 5,000 men when Londoners reached the rebel lines.

Before this new army arrived, however, most of the rebels had already dissipated. A few had remained, still standing about the king, still speaking to him about the ills of the kingdom. When these men discovered that the open area of the plain was beginning to be filled with armed men, they too decided it was time to be moving on. Without any more bloodshed the rebellion was over.

Through it all, the fourteen-year-old king had met the crisis with amazing coolness and courage. He related later that he never felt himself in any real danger, that the rebels had not blamed him for the death of their leader and that they treated him with respect at all times. Nevertheless, the action of Richard on that day was a test of true courage that few kings in the history of England could come close to matching.

For a moment, it seemed as if all of England had a leader in which it could be proud. But that early promise was not to be fulfilled. In later years King Richard proved to be extravagant, unjust, and faithless. Outside of his actions in the peasant's revolt, his only good act was to terminate the struggle with France. His biggest mistake, however, was his insistence to abandon Parliamentary government. With the Magna Carta being signed before Richard's reign, Parliament was now an established part of national life.

Yet, it was powers outside his control that finally put an end to Richard's rule. His reign marked the beginning of the War of the Roses. Popularly called the Cousins War, it consisted of a series of struggles for the Crown. It was to last for over a century and affected the reigns of seven English kings.

Richard was the first king to fall in this struggle. In 1399 Henry of Lancaster, soon to become Henry IV, returned from exile, deposed Richard, and was elected king by Parliament. Richard was murdered in prison in 1400 and the War of the Roses had claimed its first victim.

Henry VI (1421-1471)
He was born to fail and he did

By far the youngest English monarch to rule his nation was Henry VI, the next boy king of England. Henry was born in

Artist rendering of the crowning of Henry VI.

1421 and began his rule when he was nine months old. Turmoil in the land, invasions, and civil war had plagued the first two boy kings of England. There was little rest from similar troubles in the reign of Henry VI.

His greatest accomplishment, however, was just staying alive as long as he did. The chances of a young king surviving childhood were remote indeed, not only in England, but in many nations of the world during those times. Aunts, uncles, cousins, and younger brothers and sisters were forever battling for more power. A young king was at the mercy of those around him. For a baby still in his cradle, it was even worse. There was no way he could protect himself. Even if he wasn't murdered, a young king was also subject to injury and disease. Medical practice was not very far advanced in the middle ages.

While still in his cradle, a plan was already well along which, if one believed in black magic, would surely have ended the king's life. Eleanor Cobham, King Henry's aunt, had employed several people, including a "witch," to devise an image of wax with the same likeness of the king. While little by little they melted the wax, the outcome was to have the king's life dwindling away in like manor. It didn't and to every believer's surprise, the king remained a healthy child.

While the king's relatives jockeyed for power, scheming against one another was well underway all the while, the young king was taking his first steps. Later, he even uttered his first words without anyone, save the young king's nurses, ever noticing or caring.

At one point even the bishop of the church, who should have been concerned with the nation's religious duties, became involved instead in a plot to kidnap the young king. The bishop employed several men to invade London and take away the young king by force. Word leaked out about the plot before the actual attack occurred, however. Chains were placed across the southern end of London Bridge to curb the attack. A great many Londoners flocked to the bridge to de-

Windsor Castle: Birthplace of Henry VI.

fend their king against the kidnappers.

The bishop's determined effort to capture the king was not without cause, however. There had been for some time a massive power struggle with the result that the king's care, it was believed, was in unscrupulous hands. The confrontation at London Bridge could have erupted into a bloody battle had not it been for cooler heads. A parley was held and it was agreed that the attack should be abandoned.

Remarkably, the young king grew out of the baby and toddler years without a scratch. By the time he was nine years old he started to take an interest in the affairs of state. A nobleman who was serving as his tutor in governmental matters reported at that time that the king had "grown in years, in statue of his person, and also in conceit and knowledge of his royal estate."

He added that the king grudged any chastising, was headstrong, and unruly. He at times was even growing impatient with those trusted to attend to the nation's business. In the end, however, he trained his pupil to be a good man and a refined gentleman, but he could not teach him kingship. This was despite the fact that from an early age he was made to appear at public functions and take his place in Parliament.

In spite of all odds, Henry VI survived his infancy, his teens, and young adulthood. As the years passed, the young

king had grown tall and deeply religious. He preferred spending long hours kneeling in prayer to the rigors of hunting or
sports. He was a loner, seldom speaking of his inner thoughts.
Because of this there was debate on whether the king was un-
usually brilliant with a wide-ranging intelligence or a simple-
ton who could barely tell right from wrong.

Often Henry seemed to be an ideal monarch, totally out of
character with his times, which were downright brutal. He
shed his kingly clothes and wore those often owned by farmers. Gentle, naïve, chase, even prudish, he was truthful almost
to a fault. He never made a promise he didn't keep and never
knowingly did an injury to anyone. He abhorred all forms of
bloodshed, which in his time was often an everyday and public spectacle. He frequently inter-
vened to spare the lives of criminals
and traitors. He even pardoned nobles who had conspired against his
own life.

Despite it all, Henry VI was ill
prepared to move the kingdom forward. He could never find success
in holding the various factions of
his government in control. He could
not curtail a civil war that raged
endlessly on during his term. At the
end of his many defeats was still
another – his total takedown as the
ruler of his country, his imprisonment, and his mysterious death in
the Tower of London.

Henry VI was but fifty years old.
He had been a very saintly man.

**Margaret of Anjou,
spouse of Henry VI**

But from his beginning in the royal
bedchamber nothing good was expected. He had fought an
uphill battle and lost.

Edward V
(1470-1483)
It's not how he lived, but how he died

Edward V

Edward V was officially King of England for just two months. He was twelve years old at the time. In any other situation it would be hardly long enough for historians to write about. More than likely he would have been quickly forgotten. But the reign of Edward V was far from normal. And nobody, it seems, has forgotten.

Over the years few knew, or even seem to care about Edward V himself. What all were concerned about, however, is what happened to Edward V. All indications show that he (then about thirteen years old) and his younger brother (about ten) were probably murdered. Despite the fact that there has always been only two main suspects, which of the two ordered the deed has plagued historians ever since.

Born in 1470, Edward V ascended to the throne in 1483. He took his coronation seriously, as befitting a monarch, but he did not live to attend it. The one to interfere with it all was his uncle, Richard, Duke of Gloucester. He had young Edward and his brother, Richard, Duke of York, removed from their mother and sent to the royal palace in the Tower of London. It wasn't long afterwards that the uncle seized the throne as Richard III on the grounds that the two boys were illegitimate. The king's marriage to the boys' mother was invalid, he said.

The palace at which the two boys were living was now

turned into a prison. At first there was still some freedom. Edward, for instance, was seen several times running about with his brother on the Tower green, playing with his bow and arrows. Those days, however, were limited.

When the news of their uncle seizing the throne was brought to him, Edward felt instinctively that his life was in danger. Attempts to comfort him failed to lift his despair. Being both clever and thoughtful beyond his years, his fears were soon justified. It wasn't long before he was taken with his brother into the inner apartments of the Tower proper. There, servants were not allowed to visit them. And day by day they began to be seen more rarely beyond the bars and windows, till at last they ceased to be seen altogether.

Dominic Mancini, an Italian who was in London at the time, wrote that the young king, like a victim prepared for sacrifice, sought remission of his sins by daily confession and penance. This, he wrote, was because the king believed that death was facing him.

Nobody knows for sure just how or when the two boys were killed. It was said from one source, however, that the boys were killed by suffocation late one evening. This was under the orders of King Richard III. Another source says it was not Richard, but King Henry (who reigned after Richard) who killed the two princes. It was said by the later source that Richard, since he was king already, had no reason to kill the two boys. On the other hand, Henry, who took the throne following the death of Richard just two years later, did.

Unfortunately, there was not enough proof to convict either man in any fair court of law. The true story will probably never be known. What is known is that the two boys were killed. This was confirmed 200 years after their death when workmen demolishing an old staircase that led from the White Tower to the adjoining King's lodging came upon a wooden chest. The chest was buried ten feet underground under a stone staircase. Whoever buried it didn't want the chest to be found.

As might be supposed, the chest contained the bones of two individuals, both children. At that time Charles II was king of England. And his chief surgeon examined the remains and declared them to be more or less the same age as the princes who were long believed to have been murdered. A suitable monument was ordered and the bones were reinterred in Westminster Abby.

Years later, in 1933, it was decided that then, with the benefit of modern science, the bones should be reexamined. This was done by an eminent physician and an cminent dentist. Thirty years later, in 1963, the examination was done again – this time by equally distinguished anthropologists and orthodontists. In both later observations, there was no reason given to dispute the conclusion reached years before. The bones, more likely than not, were those of the two brothers.

Ludlow Castle was a home of Edward V.

Edward VI (1537-1553)
He was the nice little boy
who loved people

It was three weeks after the death of Henry VIII on Saturday, February 19, 1547, that nine-year-old Edward VI (Henry and his third wife Jane Seymour's young son) rode out from the Tower of London to Westminster Abbey. It was the day for the new king's coronation and much of England had assembled along the route to welcome the boy.

He was dressed in white velvet, decorated with Venetian silver, diamonds, rubies, and pearls. On his head was a white velvet cap. His horse, a huge stallion, was caparisoned in crimson satin and embroidered with pearls and gold. By each side rode three knights. Behind him were members of the royal family, courtiers, clergymen, foreign emissaries, halberdiers, and simple yeoman. It was a day all would remember.

As the procession slowly went through sixteenth-century English streets, cannons boomed, church bells rang, and choirs sang from mounted settings as Edward passed. Musicians played and children sang and recited in unison – "Hail noble Edward, our king and sovereign…"

Crowds lined several abreast along the way as each minor official, guild, and neighboring church participated in some appropriate ceremony. When the procession reached the Cross at Chepe, the lord mayor gave a short address, and in the city's tradition with new kings, handed the boy a large purse containing a thousand marks of gold.

What wasn't calculated, however, was the fact the purse was far too heavy for the young boy to hold. While the boy was giving thanks for the gift, it was gradually slipping out of his hands. Noting the predicament the young king was in, the captain of the guard assisted him with the heavy bundle. The procession then continued.

Edward VI at age nine.

Already well behind schedule, the young king stopped everything to a halt once again when he caught sight of a Spanish rope dancer. The man was descending from a rope which was stretched from the spire of St. Paul's Cathedral down to the Deanery Gate. Without using hands or legs, the performer glided down the rope on his breast like an arrow from a bow. When he reached the ground he came to the king and kissed the small boy's feet. The man then went back up the rope and continued to perform more feats while young Edward watched spellbound.

The urging of those around Edward that the hour was late and the procession should continue was to no avail. When the group did continue it was well into the late hours and by the time the group reached the Palace of Westminster it was nearly dark.

The coronation was held the next morning in Westminster Abbey. It was official: Edward VI was now king of England. At his coronation, however, Edward was given even more responsibilities than had been given to others before him. Besides the title of king of England, he was crowned the supreme head of the church. Now, not only was Edward responsible for his subjects' bodies, but their souls as well.

After the coronation, Edward presided at a banquet in Westminster Hall, his crown still on his head. And even though he was just nine years old, Edward took up his new burdens aware that he must answer to God and history for any mistakes. His training was to this end. In his own mind he was prepared, even eager to get to work.

Among his duties was to attend council meetings, receive foreign ministers, even listen to complaints of citizens. Another duty was to knight those who had accomplished some feat for the kingdom. He took no particular pleasure in knighting people. Yet there was one time, when it became a most enjoyable game.

The subject of the knighting was Throckmorton, the younger son of an impoverished squire. Throckmorton became particularly attached to Edward. Because of this close friendship, Throckmorton would never treat Edward as the king, but as a schoolboy friend. When he visited he would take Edward aside, amusing him with absurd stories and crude humor. Edward, tired of the stuffiness of the lords and officials at the palace, always looked forward to his friend's visits.

One day, however, after returning from a knighting ceremony for somebody he didn't know, Edward looked at Throckmorton, whom he did know, and drew his sword. "Kneel," he said. "I will knight thee Sir Nicholas Throckmorton."

Throckmorton did not want to be knighted. He walked backwards for a while across the big room, and then turned and ran through the various chambers of the palace. Edward,

Artist rendering of Edward VI holding court.

with sword raised and bursting with laughter, gave chase through hallways and passages, past guards and palace servants. At last, Throckmorton hid himself in a cupboard. The king, guessing what he had done, flung open the door. Throckmorton looked up in amazement as Edward placed his sword on Throckmorton's shoulder. "I proclaim thee a knight," Edward said.

Even though Edward was the king, his age demanded that he have some help with the task of governing. The chore of ruling the land was just too great. His uncle, the Duke of Somerset, became "protector." As a protector, however, he was a failure. Northumberland, a schemer with unbridled ambition, then became the strong man. He too was more of a problem than a help. The country was in turmoil. It was marked with social unrest that erupted into riot and rebellion. During this time Edward exerted more and more of his powers. And the king, even as a boy, was obeyed.

For the most part Edward had high ideals. At times he was heard criticizing the harsh actions of his father. He felt many of the laws of England at that time were unjust. He wanted change. As a guide, Edward, at age thirteen, wrote a directive he titled, "A Discourse about the Reformation of Many Abuses." It detailed abuses and called for reformation. It included providing good education and good laws which would be executed justly without respect of persons. It called for good examples of rulers, the punishing of vagabonds and idle persons, and encouraging the good. It also called for friendship in all parts of the commonwealth.

Edward thought it best that the great noblemen should return to their own lands, there to see that the statutes are fully and duly executed. Unfortunately, few of the ideals were realized in Edward's reign. What was done was that he initiated some reform in religious practice. The real landmark of his reign – the writing of the *Book of Common Prayer* – is probably what the ages will credit him most.

For more than 400 years, this piece of literature has been a

**Copy of Edward VI's Book of
Common Prayer published in 1596.**

mainstay in the church. As a work of art it has stood alongside the works of the great sixteenth century poets and dramatists. The young king was actively involved in the book's preparation. As part of his contribution, Edward wrote the order of service for the Knights of the Garter, making three drafts, one in Latin and two in English. With the *Book of Common Prayer* came uniformity of worship throughout the land. The book also helped turn England into a Protestant state.

Being the leader of the church and king of his country was no small task for Edward. And yet he still had time for his studies and retained in himself a constant reminder that he was still a boy. For heads of state this mixture was somewhat hard to take. For instance, when Edward felt he had enough of the stately things he would leave the castle for more delightful endeavors. When a foreign minister requested an audience, he would be told the king has "gone out to play." Often these same ministers had to pursue him into the woods, the tennis courts, or play yard. And there, while Edward was tossing a ball back and forth to a friend, he would be interviewed.

Edward's upbringing also taught him how to deal with people, the powerful and those who opposed his rule. When he showed anger or self-will his tutors would often remind him who he was. Among this instruction was that "every fault is greater in a king than in a mere man." He was also taught that he must be "slow to judge and be willing to hear all men." He was told that he should second guess his own reason. He was also not to appear as all knowing, but follow what Socrates said in his old age, that as a man he –"knoweth only this thing, that he knew nothing."

Often Edward would put this learning to good use. Once, when Bishop Ridley gave a heated sermon concerning the conditions of the poor in London, the bishop lashed out at those in authority (in this case the king) who did nothing.

Following the sermon a messenger was sent to the bishop with the message that the king wanted to see him. The bishop was taken to a large room in the palace. It was empty of people. In the center of the room were two chairs. As the bishop waited, expecting the worst, Edward came into the room alone. The bishop sank to his knees but Edward insisted that he get up and put on his cap. The king then sat down and asked the bishop to do the same. He said that they were alone at his command. And that no formalities were to be observed.

Instead of condemning the bishop, possibly having him imprisoned, Edward thanked the bishop for his fine sermon. He read out some of the notes he had made of it, which was somewhat lengthy, all the while the bishop sat amazed and speechless. Edward then got to the part where the bishop spoke out about the poor, thanking him again for his comments, all the while the bishop remained unable to speak.

In the end, Edward said he agreed with the bishop. The king had indeed neglected the poor. He said from that day on the poor would be taken care of and asked the bishop if he would help him devise a plan whereby that could be done.

For a while, the slight, fair boy and the bearded, elderly bishop sat looking at each other, neither speaking a word. It was the dream of the bishop that such a concern for the poor take place, but never did he dream it would come about like this. When the bishop did regain his speech, the king sent for a secretary and dictated a letter on the spot commanding the lord mayor's immediate attendance to the matter. The king then gave orders that the letter be delivered at once. With this Edward stood up, extended his hand in friendship, and left the room.

In the weeks that followed the bishop met with the lord mayor and worked out a plan whereby help was on its way for the poor. Historians pretty much agree that Edward had the makings of one of the best kings England had ever known. He was the nice little boy who loved people. He even kept a little dog in a basket in his bedroom.

He honored and respected those who were assigned to teach him not only his kingly chores, but also philosophy, geometry, and the foreign languages French, Spanish, and Italian. He even honored those who taught him music to the point that he excelled in playing the flute. He particularly liked those who taught him geography, which spurred as a hobby he had of collecting globes and maps.

For the most part, the young king was fair minded. But Edward lived in hard times. He was often cold and calculating, not unlike his ancestors and not unlike the cold and calculating times in which he lived.

Unfortunately, England would never know exactly what Edward would have accomplished, what new directions he would have sent his country. For in Edward's fourteenth year he came down with a sickness, which historians expect was measles or smallpox. This was followed by other illnesses in the months to come. Then, quite suddenly at age sixteen, King Edward VI died. It was later determined the cause of death was tuberculosis. This was brought about due to his earlier health problems that suppressed his natural immunity to the disease.

Edward left this world with many of his dreams unrealized and he left a country torn by opposing factions. And with Edward, England said goodbye to the last of its boy kings.

FRANCE TODAY

CHAPTER 4
FRANCE

For the past several centuries, France has been a major power in the world. From its inception it has expanded its boundaries, built and maintained a large army, has been a major force on the high seas, and has played a major part in colonizing other lands. In fact, there are few areas in Europe, North and South America, Asia, and Africa where France hasn't played a significant part in each continent's history.

There were close to a dozen boy kings in France, those who took over the reins of their country while under the age of fourteen. In their ranks were some of Frances greatest rulers. Louis XIV became king when he was just five years old. He ruled for seventy-two years and became Europe's longest reigning monarch.

France's boy kings were also some of the more interesting rulers. One developed the habit of sitting under a tree by the side of the road and talked to all who passed by. He also enjoyed attending services in churches so humble that they lacked seats. He was later to be proclaimed St. Louis. Another boy king was once chased from the royal kitchen for snitching food after mealtime. He enjoyed playing hide-and-seek in the towers, chambers, and passageways of the Louvre and pushing a girlfriend around the gardens in a wheelbarrow.

Little is known concerning the first two boy kings of France. The first was King Lothair, son of Louis IV who was born in 941 and came to the throne of France in 954 when he was thirteen years old. He ruled for twenty-two years, dying in 906 at the age of thirty-five.

It was nearly a century later when France's next boy ruler came to power. His name was King Philip I, son of Henry I. He was just eight years old when he became king in 1060. He remained on the throne for forty-eight years, dying in 1108.

Lothair (941-986) No dull moments here with battles, family feuds

Lothair, at the age of thirteen, was crowned at Rheims in the presence of several feudal lords. From the beginning Lothair wanted to rule alone and reinforced his authority.

Lothair

All was not well in the land. Lothair inherited a fragmented kingdom where the great magnates took lands, rights, and offices almost without any regard for the authority of the king. And so from the very beginning Lothair was deeply involved in the many affairs designed to have the royal power reestablished.

His early years were devoted to wars against the vassals, particularly against the Duke of Normandy. It started just a year after he became king. That is when Lothair, at the age of fourteen, set out to conquer Aquitaine. His armies, however, didn't have a great deal of success and after just two months on the battlefield, Lothair headed home.

On his way he was attacked by Guillaume of Poitiers. Here, Lothair's army was victorious and Lothair came back at least a partial hero.

Throughout his years as the king, wars occupied much of Lothair's time. When he wasn't fighting with the outside world, he was in the middle of family feuds.

There was a lighter story, floating around at the time, which became one of the most interesting events in history. In one of Lothair's travels about Europe, he made an unexpected visit to the city of Aachen, a border town in Germany known for its warm mineral springs. Here, Emperor Otto II the Red of Germany was about to sit down to an elaborate dinner that had been prepared for him. Not ready to do battle with his enemy, the king of France, Otto ducked out a back door. Lothair then sat down at the table and ate the dinner that had been prepared for Otto.

For that embarrassing moment, Otto, who was also Lothair's cousin, vowed that he would return the "favor" by doing more battle with France. Beneath the walls of Paris, he said he would sing to him such a Halleluiah as the king had never heard. It was a boast that was actually carried out months later.

Emperor Otto, after ravaging the countryside around Rheims, arrived with an army of 60,000 men at the walls of Paris. A lance was thrown that stuck to the walls of the city. And then Otto did sing his Halleluiah, his men joining in on the chorus. But that was it.

After that, King Otto and his men turned around and went home. Later, despite their many differences, peace was made between the two rulers. Lothair died in 906 at the age of forty-five. His son Louis V succeeded him .

Lothair leading his army into battle.

Philip I pictured with his wife.

Philip I (1052-1108)
The king who fell victim
to a bad press

Every once in a while rulers go down in history as heroes. Others, who may not be as well liked, get tagged as bad guys. Such was the case of Philip I. For many years he was the victim of a bad press. Several historians have condemned him for one thing or another. In their sight he just didn't match up to what a king should be. Now that prejudices have worn off and thoughts are a little clearer, Philip I is seen as not such a bad guy after all.

Philip I was only seven years old when he succeeded his father as king of France. At first he was under the regency of his mother and Baldwin V of Flanders which lasted only until he was fourteen, when he gained full control. At the time the monarchy was extremely weak, but he grew up as an efficiently unscrupulous king who made the best of the monarchy's weak position. In the end, however, he succeeded in adding to the royal treasury and enlarging his country's domains.

Nevertheless, almost from the very beginning, he was somewhat of an independent thinker and doer. Just because someone else got excited about something or because everyone else thought something should be done in a particular situation, this, according to Philip I, was every reason in the world not to rush the matter.

Philip saw no reason to interfere when William the Conqueror set his eyes on England. He was indifferent to the movements within the Catholic Church for reform. While all of France was in a fever of excitement prior to the crusades, Philip seemed to share none of the enthusiasm. Philip was content to do his own thing.

Meanwhile, all around him, the spirit of adventure and of conquest had taken possession of nearly every heart. France was gradually waking up from the kind of moral slumber which had weighed over it for upwards of four centuries. Philip would not, it seemed, be a part of such an awakening without much thought.

Pope Gregory VII denounced Philip as a tyrant possessed by the devil and at times called him a perjurer and a robber. Historians followed suit labeling him as one of France's worst monarchs. Philip just didn't have a chance for the history books.

In reality, Philip was a practical ruler and a realist. First he had to clean up things at home. For a good part of his reign was spent putting down revolts by some of his power-hungry nobles. Then he laid down policy and some of the foundations in which subsequent kings were honored for carrying out. His seemingly indifference to the conquest of England was due not because Philip didn't care, but because he was still very young and France probably would not have succeeded in any kind of involvement anyway. So Philip chose instead to foster dissention within the Anglo-Norman royal house. It took several years but his policy succeeded.

As for Philip's participation in the crusades, Philip just may have led the first crusade had he not been disqualified from taking part in it. This was due to the fact he was under sentence of excommunication from the church for his marriage with Bertrada de Montfort, putting aside his first marriage. Likewise, his lack of enthusiasm for church reform was due to the general danger he saw in a church independent of lay control. He felt such reform could be a menacing foe to royal power.

Philip saw no greatness of vision. He realized that the king had first to make himself master in his own house, the royal domain, before he could master his kingdom at large. In the long run it proved best for King Philip and it proved best for France.

Louis IX (Saint Louis)
(1214-1270)
He was the most respected
and well liked of all monarchs

In 1226, when little Louis IX came to the throne of France, he was just twelve years old. He ruled not the France we know today, but a divided one. His brothers and important nobles held pieces of it as did the king of England and the king of Spain.

Growing up, tutors taught him Latin, public speaking, writing, military arts, government, and geography. Experienced horsemen taught him riding and the fine points of

Statue of Louis IX.

hunting. All of this was while his mother trained him to be a great leader and a good Christian. At first, as regent, she had the final say when he was young, but within a couple of years he took over the decision-making and she became his close advisor.

One of Louis's first undertakings, after he became king, was to sell off all the precious stones and jewelry owned by the royal family. This was done to provide funds for the founding of a new abbey to be known as Royaumont. While it was being built and after, he would come over from his castle at Asnieres to help the monks, carrying stones and mortar as they did. The abbey filled an important place in Louis's

Royaumont Abbey

life. It was always one of his favorite refuges, a spiritual home where he could join the monks in their exercise of piety.

Here he shed the responsibilities and ceremonies of kingship to serve the monks with his own hands. He was especially kind to a Brother Leger, who suffered from a grievous skin disease, now generally considered to be leprosy. The sick monk was kept in a separate house away from the others. He was avoided and shunned by all about him. The king not only insisted on visiting the monk but cut and served his food. He even brought special delicacies from the royal kitchen.

When the time was right the young king set about to bring peace and unity to his country. This he did by persuading his nobles to end a good deal of their quarreling. He also persuaded England and Spain to give up their holdings in France. And then he found time to lead two crusades in an attempt to bring the holy city of Jerusalem back into the control of the Christian community.

Everywhere he went as well as at home he set standards of honesty and integrity. None of this was typical of kings and rulers in that period. His devotion to the suffering of others was one of the most unique features of the young king. In his frequent visits to hospitals he took pleasure in personal ministry to the sick. When some were more ill than others, he was the more ready to wait on them. He knelt before them and cut up their bread and meat. He placed the morsel already cut in their mouths, and then wiped them with a napkin.

In other things, the young king avoided all improper games and kept himself from all unseemly or dishonorable things. He injured no one by word or deed and always addressed those to whom he spoke with respect. Once, while still a boy, he developed the habit of sitting under a tree by the side of the road. Here he would talk to all who passed by. He also enjoyed attending services in churches so humble that they lacked seats.

One morning, when he was still quite young, a number of beggars were waiting in the palace courtyard. It was early and everyone in the palace was still sleeping. King Louis, however, saw the beggars from his window, quickly dressed in simple clothing, and came down the palace stairs. With the help of a servant he carried a large bag filled with coins. Then he

Louis IX pays his respects to the Pope.

began to distribute the coins to the beggars. He gave the largest amounts to those who seemed to be the neediest.

When he returned to his room he was met by a monk who was astonished at what he had just seen. Explaining, the young king said it was the people who he should serve and not they him. "They fight for me by their prayers against all my enemies and maintain peace in the kingdom. I have not yet paid them the salary that is due."

He commanded troops by the time he was fifteen. Even in battle the king had a way about him quite different from other leaders. Once, when a castle was stormed and won by the king, the enemy soldiers were taken prisoner. The leader was the son of a ruler not present in the land during the time of the battle. Regardless, it was the custom in those days to put to death all the prisoners. When the king was asked when the executions should take place, they were astonished to learn that he would authorize no executions.

"The young man," the king said, "does not deserve death because he obeyed his father's order, nor do his men for faithfully serving their lord." With this, the king had all of the prisoners put into a place of safety.

Voltaire, one of the great historians-philosophers, said of Louis IX that he was a prince destined to reform Europe, had it been capable of being reformed. He said Louis was the one, if anyone, to bring France up as a model for the rest of mankind. Unfortunately future leaders of France would not make that come to pass. Voltaire reasoned that it was not in the ability of one man, no matter how noble, to bring about such a departure from tradition.

In 1270, at the age of sixty-eight, Louis IX died. France would never be the same. In 1297, seven years after his death, the leaders of the Catholic Church gathered together and proclaimed the dead king a saint. He was dedicated to his church, to peace, and to helping his subjects and maintaining his kingdom. As such Louis IX was one of the most respected and well liked of all absolute monarchs in history.

Charles VI (1368-1422)
All of France loved its mad king

Charles VI

Charles VI as both a boy and man loved to disguise himself in peasant clothes and run about the countryside. He would visit the marketplaces, join in games, crash parties, and visit inns and taverns. He would question residents as to their views. And, then not knowing who he was, he even asked what they thought of the king. For Charles VI all of this was great fun.

At first, as a young boy, Charles was viewed to be a promising king. He was said to be a dreamy, sentimental, agreeable, and pleasure-loving boy. In his later years he became mad. For prolonged periods he took upon himself the names and positions of others, actually believing he was not the king of France. He danced when there was no dance or dance partners. There were periods of violence when he tore down curtains, broke drinking cups, and threw chairs and books at whatever suited him.

Because of this, the doors leading from his apartments were nailed shut so that he could run wild in this small enclosure. This he could do without endangering himself or others. Following his periods of violence there was a time of fear when he would sit huddled motionless in the corner of his room. He thought he was made of glass and might break at any moment. At other times he feared evil spirits were after him. For this he would pile furniture before his door, barricading himself in against them.

The king, however, was not completely mad. Those spells would pass and he would become normal once again. One never knew when or where a new episode would occur. Although mad, his madness was regarded by all as harmless. The common people actually enjoyed the times when in public the king would engage in some folly. Throughout his reign his popularity steadily increased.

But the king did not always have it so well. There were some real problems. And quite understandably so, the people were not always so devoted to their king. From the beginning, part of this was due to high taxes and corruption in government. It seemed to be a way of life in France when Charles, at age eleven, became king.

What he inherited was a country in turmoil and still in what later was to be called The Hundred Years' War. The people, expecting something better when Charles was crowned, were sadly disappointed to learn that Charles' uncles were, in the beginning, in control. They were leading the young king in the direction which best suited their respective interests.

Charles' maternal uncle, Louis Duc de Bourbon, was responsible for the personal care of the king. Although young Charles was given the best education a medieval prince could expect, it wasn't adequate. The uncle was more interested in going about pillaging the country from end to end. And when it was all over, he marched off laden with treasure.

Another uncle, Philippe le Hardi Duc de Bourgogne, didn't do much better. He and another uncle, the Duc de Berri, spent much of their time trying to curtail a revolution of the people. Citizens everywhere were protesting their high taxes and the cruel treatment these uncles had placed upon the land.

As far as an education, Charles was taught little more than how to scrawl his own name in ungainly pot-hooks. He was, however, taught war. He was taken with a strong army into Flanders, and there on the field of Rosebeke, Charles was allowed to give the sign that preceded the slaughter of 26,000 Flemish citizens. They were but half-armed merchants and shopkeepers protesting the tyrannical and inefficient rule of Count Louis de Male.

Charles was told that it was the duty of kings to go to the aid of their fellow rulers and in this case, it was only right that the French army come to the aid of the count. When it was all over, young Charles was taken for a ride over the battlefield where laid the thousands of Flemish dead. Here, he was told, he was indeed a great king. He was not told that the battle was fought not just to aid the count, but to help secure the land for an eventual takeover by Charles' uncle.

So that the uncles could do as they wished, Charles, still a young boy, was taught to sleep when he should have been at his council table and to go about the business of being a king when he should have been asleep.

At sixteen years of age, he was married to the fourteen-year-old Isabeau of Bavaria. Unknown to Charles, even this was brought about to secure some political ground for Charles' power-hungry uncle Philippe. But as soon as he met his future wife he was smitten and demanded that the marriage was held immediately. It was, and the marriage for the first few years was a happy one. And that was despite the fact that Isabeau could not speak French and had no interest in learning it, and Charles never understood German.

Charles, however, wasn't ignorant of all the problems his uncles were causing the people. He went along with much of it only because he didn't have a choice. He thought the time was just not right even though legally he should have taken full control of the government when he turned fourteen years of age.

All of that changed when Charles believed enough was enough. Now, twenty years old and with the help of Pierre Arcelin de Montaigu, cardinal of Laon, Charles finally announced he was going to rule alone. At a public gathering he thanked his uncles for the job they had done and suggested that their services were needed elsewhere in the kingdom. Reluctantly, the uncles relinquished their power.

Charles was ill prepared to govern. He was impatient and not accepting advice. He was incapable of serious thought, light in in morals, and lighter still in a sound mind. He took no thought about money, spending great amounts on whims rather than on real needs.

Charles also was not all that innocent. Even as a young boy he readily took part, even ordered the sacking of towns and villages. After the battle at Roosebecke his blood-thirstiness was comparable to his uncles. More often than not he gave little thought to the suffering of his people. He did not fully believe that their revolts were indeed justified.

Despite such a background, the government Charles had now formed was not totally bad. Several wars were ended with truces. Problems with the church were resolved. Taxes were reduced and a system of justice established. With this, the king thought he was free to lead a life of absolute folly. He held tournaments and balls and celebrations of all kinds. When there was no reason for a celebration or a gathering, he invented one.

He thought it might be nice to hold a state funeral. When nobody of notoriety died he gave a most expensive and lavish funeral for the famous Breton warrior, Bertrand du Guesclin, who had already been dead for four years.

The king also thought it might be nice to welcome his bride, Queen Isabeau, into Paris. Since their marriage five years earlier, she had entered Paris hundreds of times. Her "first entry" was nevertheless celebrated with every symbol of pomp and magnificence. There were dances, music making, plays, and celebration of all kinds. The king, not waiting for all the action to come to him, went to it. Disguised as a city lad, he roamed the streets to watch the queen's procession pass by.

It was by such actions that the common people learned to love their king. And even in his later years, when his mind completely gave out, they loved him. His courtiers endeavored to keep him happy by leading him into giddy acts of folly. They even tried to cure him through methods prescribed by all the leading physicians. When that failed, they even resorted to sorcery. It was all to no avail. Based on his behavior, doctors in later times believed the king may have suffered from schizophrenia or bi-polar disorder.

Charles VI died in October 1422. Once known as Charles the Beloved, he later was called Charles the Mad. Despite this the French people grieved deeply. After all, he had reigned for more than fifty years. His funeral, however, was poorly attended by the great ones of Europe. His own family members did not attend. Of royal blood, John, Duke of Bedford was the only one and he was a foreigner.

Charles VIII
(1470-1498)
He coined the words "Let George Do It"

On the death of his father, Louis XI, a thirteen-year-old boy became king as Charles VIII. Because France at that time had fixed the age of fourteen as the age when a new king could govern by himself, the administration was left in the hands of Charles' oldest sister, twenty-three-year-old Anne de Beaujeu.

Charles VIII

Although Anne governed well and was highly thought of in all of France, the king had many failings. He was small in stature and badly proportioned. He had a large head, a big nose, and prominent lips always half open. He didn't speak that well, was barely literate, weakly, his words full of hesitation. His mind was deficient and he had few, if any, skills with the exception of athletics.

Charles was also a dreamer. He longed for an opportunity of imitating the great accomplishments of kings before him. He was constantly dreaming of expeditions to distant countries. He could often be found alone in his room, reading for hours of the exploits of others.

Weak in most respects, Charles had a difficult time with his strong-willed sister, of whom he had a wholesome terror. Although Anne had no ambitions of remaining in control and did spend much time with Charles, preparing him for the role he must eventually play, Charles seemed forever lax in his abilities. It seemed evident to most observers at that time that Charles would never be an even adequate king, let alone the kind of king Charles was forever reading about in his books.

The years went by; past the time Charles should have rightly taken over the reins of government. Charles made no move in that direction, content in letting others do all the work. He would spend his time reading, hunting, and engaging in athletic contests with his friends. He did not, it seemed, want to challenge the rule of his sister. So there he remained for many years under the thumb of Anne.

Then something happened to change all that. It started when one man, Cardinal Georges d'Amboise, needed a favor. And to see this favor granted the man had a plan. He would approach Charles (then twenty years of age) and convince him that enough was enough. The king, according to this plan, could assert his authority in a way that would release him from the position he was in. At the same time it would not require the king to face his sister. In so many words it would tell her he was taking on all of the responsibilities of being king.

All Charles had to do, according to the cardinal, was to lead a small band of men to Bourges and there, with his royal hand, release the Duke of Orleans. The duke, considered by Charles a good friend, was being held prisoner by Anne. The duke was next in line (after Charles) to the throne. He was a brother-in-law to Charles and Anne by virtue of his marriage to their young sister Jeanne.

Anne de Beaujeu

When presenting the plan to Charles, the cardinal said by

releasing the duke, Charles would prove that he was a king and put Anne in her place. Enchanted with the idea, Charles did just that. It was his first act of authority and it worked. King Charles was now definitely released from the domination of his sister.

Georges d'Amboise, the man with the plan, was later to become prime minister to the duke who in turn became the king of France as Louis XII. So able and versatile was George that whenever something needed done the people would merely say, "Laissez faire a George" from whence our saying, "Let George do it," originates.

Within a year, Charles would marry the fourteen-year-old Anne, Duchess of Brittany, thus merging France with Brittany. The king then set his eyes on the Kingdom of Naples, bringing up the fine print of an old document that Naples had been bequeathed to Charles' father, Louis XI. Although the present ruler of Naples, Ferdinand of Arragon, was there for as vague of a reason as the claim of Charles, Ferdinand had one advantage. He was there first. In thirteenth-century Europe this was nine tenths of the law. Regardless, Charles set out in the hopes that Naples would be the first of many conquests.

Thousands of men on both sides died in the battles that followed. In the end, Charles was forced to leave conquered lands and return to France, the Naples adventure a failure.

Later, back in France, Charles was hastening to the tennis court one morning and, forgetting to duck, struck his head against a low archway. Within a day the king was dead. He was just twenty-eight years old.

Charles did not obtain the accomplishments of other kings, as he had long dreamed. Nor was he the king he admired so among others in history. In most respects he was a failure. But from the beginning, nothing much was expected.

Charles IX (1550-1574)
His reign started off bad
and got worse

Charles IX

When Charles IX began his reign, he wept. He was just ten years old. The coronation ceremony was five hours long. The weight of his crown was just too much. As Charles IX lay dying, just fourteen years later, he wept again. This time it was for his disastrous days as king.

The problem really rested with his mother, Catherine de Madici, who ruled France as queen regent for the next three years until Charles was thirteen. A strong and powerful woman, Catherine had a strange and unnatural relationship with her young son. She hardly let him out of her sight. She even insisted that he sleep in her bedroom at night. "No alien influence should steal this king from me in his boyhood," she said.

As a child, Charles was described as having a narrow rat-like face and a sly expression. He had a birthmark between his nose and upper lip. He was taught to paint, sketch, write verse, and carve wood. His lessons included history and languages like Latin and Greek. Although he took no pleasure in studying, it was said he did so only to please his mother.

For Charles there was plenty to do while growing up. Raised with his siblings, the royal family often went by barge, visiting other nobles in their castles and country estates. At home there was a group of acrobats who were hired to entertain the children. Outside there was a walled garden where Charles and his friends could play. There was even a small zoo that held wolves, wild boars, lion cubs, a bear, and an assortment of small animals from Africa.

There was even an extended trip when Charles turned fourteen that took the family away from Paris, visiting communities throughout France. Then, back home, Charles led a mock naval battle and in winter got into snowball fights. There were even some pranks. Once when his mother was meeting with an official from the Vatican, Charles and his friends dressed up as bishops and riding donkeys, burst into the room.

At the same time, all was not well with Charles. As he got a little older not only did his health deteriorate, but he became mentally unstable. Sensitive and high-strung, Charles IX was often stubborn and could easily be driven into a hysterical frenzy. His mother was just as persistent and could almost always cajole him into doing just what she wanted him to do.

It was a time in France that Protestants and Catholics were at odds. The Protestants (Huguenots) were seeking an end to what they believed were real problems within the Catholic Church. At the same time the Catholics felt the Huguenots were a threat to the established religion.

Quarreling soon led to fighting and then killing. One bad incident led to another. Wild rumors spread across the land. It was not a pleasant time.

When Admiral Coligny, the leader of the Protestants, began to make frequent visits, a fondness grew between the boy king and the admiral. Catherine, however, felt that the admiral was getting much too close. She thought he commanded an undue amount of influence over the boy king.

To change all of that she lavished upon the wild rumors of the young boy's planned assassination. This, according to the stories she told, was in the planning by the Huguenots. She made certain that every gory detail of the rumor was related to Charles so that his sympathies would lie once again with the Catholics.

The badgering continued and continued until one day in a terrified rage the boy yelled out, "If you kill the admiral, kill all the Huguenots in France, so that none shall be left to reproach me after it is done!" Running from the room he screamed, "Let them all be killed! Let them all be killed."

The Catholics figured this was the go-ahead they needed to make it all legal. And on August 24, 1572, mobs raged throughout Paris. Huguenots everywhere were dragged from their homes and killed. Those even suspected to have Huguenot leanings were met with the same treatment. It made no difference to the mobs if the persons they killed were men, women, or children. All were to die.

From Paris the killing spread to other cities. Soon the entire nation was red with the blood of those who merely believed differently. When it was all over it was estimated at the time that some 100,000 people were killed. Modern historians, however, put this number at about 7,000. Whatever the actual figure was, there was nothing like it in the memory of the Western world at that time and there would be nothing like it again, maybe not until the atrocities of Nazi Germany during World War II.

There were many French families who were horrified by what was occurring. They even risked their lives by hiding their friends of the reformed faith. Many French citizens, however, seemed to approve of the killings. They were saying that henceforward there would be but one religion in all France. Joining in that approval was Spain and the church in Rome. All other nations condemned the killings as butchery. Even Ivan the Terrible of Russia, certainly far from a saint himself, lodged a protest.

In 1574, the king, suffering from tuberculosis, had a hemorrhage of the lungs. Shortly thereafter he died at the age of twenty-four. He was not a great king. He did little for France. For King Charles the end came only with regrets on how miserably he managed the kingdom. He suffered bitter remorse for the part he had in the killing of thousands of French citizens, only because of their religious beliefs. He rejoiced only to the fact he left no heir to his monstrous heritage.

GROWING UP IN ENGLAND AND FRANCE

Medieval times in England and France were not healthy periods for children. Due to unsanitary conditions, a lack of immunity to disease and other factors, twenty-five percent of all children would die in their first year. Of those that survived, twelve percent more would succumb between the ages of one and four. Then for six percent of those survivors between the ages of five and nine, their lives as well would end.

Peasant homes, mostly small cottages, had small windows and were often dark and gloomy. And because of inclement weather conditions, they had to share what little space they had with various farm animals. To make matters worse, and because they cooked inside over an open fire, and with little ventilation, their homes were often smoky.

For play, children participated in board games such as chess and checkers indoors, and outside in games of hide and seek, tag, see saw, walking on stilts, or swimming in ponds or rivers.

Louis XIII (1601-1643)
This boy king liked his toy soldiers

Louis XIII

In France the king-to-be or the next in line for kingship should he still be young, is called a dauphin. From the time he was born until he was eight years old Louis XIII knew no other name. Although his father was very much alive and still king of France, the dauphin was respected and loved as the ruler-to-be.

When he was but a month old, his public life began with a state entry into Paris. Here he not only received the city fathers, but held two more receptions. It was at the old palace of St. Germain-en-Laye that he remained for four years.

A healthy, good-tempered, and active child, Louis enjoyed meeting people and treated them all alike whether they were noblemen, foreign envoys, market women, or shopkeepers. The queen never hugged or kissed him, never even picked him up. His father, however, would play with him by the hour. His father would even take Louis with him to his various assignments as king, meeting envoys, watching parades, and reviewing the troops.

His upbringing followed the pattern of the time. It was a combination of barbarity and culture, of high accomplishment, brutal discipline, and crude horseplay. He was a happy child, but he grew up restless and in constant need of violent and strenuous diversion.

Years before his eighth birthday one of his favorite pastimes was playing with his toy soldiers with his young friends. He possessed a complete suit of armor and knew the names of each of the different arms. Even when alone, the dauphin could be seen playing often in the garden; Louis walking about pulling a small toy cannon. He enjoyed a game he made up that included saving a girl playmate from a dragon. The dragon was played by a young page. Once he even built a tower out of some bricks which court builders left lying around. Later he added to that a plank from which he constructed a makeshift drawbridge.

He enjoyed drawing and painting, taking lessons from the many artisans of the court. His favorite sport, however, was falconry, which he enjoyed from the time he was a very young boy. The first hunt he himself organized was when he was but six years old. Some of his happiest hours, however, were spent in the planting and caring of his own garden, a four-square enclosure, ditched all around on which he built a small bridge.

Growing up a king was not all play, however, and Louis was being taught all along the duty of rulers. In those early years, however, he had no use for protocol and ceremony. He never enjoyed dressing up and, more often than not, didn't. Rather, he generally wore a torn shirt and grubby socks. When presented to his subjects he would mingle with them rather than take his place on a throne and be presented in a formal manner. Every year saw more responsibilities. He received envoys at more frequent intervals. By age seven, he was already attending council meetings.

Young Louis had his problems. As a child he was seen as very sickly and used to stammer extensively. Consequently he spoke little. But his "sickness" was questionable. Observers saw him as a hypochondriac who always believed he was ill. At the same time, when involved in something he really liked to do, the "sickness" disappeared.

All of this training was not too soon. For one day while he went about his daily chores he received an urgent summons from the queen. Taken to the Louvre, he ran up the stairs, through the confusion of voices and footsteps, to his father's bedroom. Here he saw a figure lying on the bed. Many people were all around. But his mother, seeing him at the door, rushed towards him saying, "The king is dead. The king is dead." He had been assassinated, stabbed to death while riding in a carriage through the streets of Paris.

At that moment, Louis, just nine years of age, was king of France. The country gave the new ruler little time to mourn the death of his father. There was work to be done. Ministers set about scheduling meetings and audiences. Parliament was called into session. Then, because of his age, his mother was given the authority to make decisions in his name.

Despite that, however, his duties increased. He was treated with even more respect by everyone. He was asked his opinion on important state matters. His commands were obeyed although the real power still was in the hands of his mother, a woman who few liked. Even Louis's relationship with his mother remained one of thinly disguised hostility. Many criticized her extravagance, her secret advisers, and her actions. These actions were not always in the best interest of France.

The country wouldn't have to wait long – just four years. Then, as Louis turned thirteen, he was declared of age to rule alone. His mother, terminated from all power, now served in the capacity of just an advisor, though an important one. But even that didn't last long. Due to mismanagement of the kingdom and ceaseless political intrigues brought on by his mother, her son had her exiled for a period of time, did away with her closest advisors, and brought in those he trusted.

For Louis, one of his most expected, even mandatory undertakings was his marriage to Anne, the daughter of Philip II of Spain. Pre-arranged years before, Louis was less than excited about the proposed marriage. For matters of State, however, it was done. Both husband and wife were just fourteen years of age. As expected the marriage was not a happy one. Anne found the king shy, sulky, and unresponsive. He flew his falcons, carved shrines, and played his guitar. He mostly ignored her. She wrote home that nothing could make her happier than to return to Spain. But that was not to happen.

The marriage, in fact, lasted. And after several stillbirths the queen finally gave birth to a son in 1638. He would be the future King Louis XIV.

As the years went on, Louis faced a series of challenges including what seemed to be opposition from all sides. He had to face several revolts, conspiracies, and rebellions that included those from his own mother and brothers. He engaged the Spanish and Habsburgs on several fronts, frequently leading his armies into battle. He even led his nation into what was to become the Thirty Years' War. Then, at the age of forty-two and long suffering from chronic ill health, he died from intestinal tuberculosis.

In the end, he may not have been the best of kings, but history puts his story in front and center. That's because the author Alexander Dumas wrote a very famous book titled *The Three Musketeers*. And this in more recent years has been turned into several motion pictures, all immortalizing King Louis XIII.

Louis XIV
(1638-1715)
This king ruled for a
long, long, long time

Born in 1638, Louis XIV had similar upbringings as most other children of royal blood. Things changed dramatically when Louis was just four years old at the death of his father. Louis was now the king of France and leader of 19 million French subjects. His mother Anne was ap-

Louis XIV

pointed regent, but the real power was in the hands of Louis's godfather, Chief Minister Cardinal Jules Mazarin. It was under Mazarin's orders that the country continued to be governed.

At the same time, Louis was being taught history, politics, and the arts, and how to conduct himself as king. He enjoyed having books read to him. When the regular studies were over he preferred spending his time fencing, dancing, and horseback riding. Much of this, however, was at the expense of a basic education. With no real studies as one would get in a regular school, what the young king learned was more practical rather than scholarly. It was enough to get by, nothing more.

While everyone went about their assigned duties, the young king himself was often neglected. Those assigned to look after him hardly knew where he was or what he was doing half the time. Once the boy narrowly escaped drowning in a pond because no one was watching him.

Handsome, athletic, and hard-working growing up, in personality he was reserved, suspicious, and secretive. Although he was polite and accomplished at ceremonial events, he had a high opinion of himself. He ate a great deal but drank little. He was religious, attending mass every day; however, he had no real interest in theology.

He was nine years old when a civil war raged in France. It not only affected the French population in general, but also the royal household. Even Louis suffered poverty, misfortune, fear, humiliation, and hunger during that time. Even though the civil disturbance ended officially in 1653 in the king's favor, Louis was greatly affected by the experience. It changed not only his character and behavior, but his mode of thought. Louis never forgave those responsible, even the common people, for the uprising.

Partly because of the civil war, the officials didn't get around to holding a formal coronation for the king until he was fifteen years old. Soon after that Louis fell in love with Mazarin's niece, Marie Mancini. The love affair lasted a good two years, but they were never allowed to get married. For political purposes, an official marriage was arranged between Louis and his first cousin, the daughter of Spain's King Philip IV.

Then, when Mazarin died in1661, Louis took on all the responsibilities of the government. Every decision made from then on was his alone.

With some seventy-two years on the throne of France, Louis XIV had a long time to do good things for his country. While he continued his predecessor's work of creating a centralized state government, he didn't do very well for his people. To begin with, he forced out those who chose to be Protestant, rather than being of Roman Catholic faith. The freedom to choose one's own religion had survived a good 150 years; but no more under Louis XIV. In addition Louis XIV seemed to want to keep a war going indefinitely somewhere or another.

During his reign France fought three major wars. These included the Franco-Dutch War, the War of the League of Augsburg, and the War of the Spanish Succession. The other conflicts included the War of Devolution and the War of Reunions. These were the lesser conflicts, but wars just the same.

When Louis died in 1715, there was no lack of potential kings to take over the government. For not only did his queen have six children (only one survived to adulthood), but there were many others, nearly a dozen children by several mistresses.

Today, France remembers its King Louis XIV as probably its most famous ruler. Remarkably, so does the United States. During his reign French explorers in North America claimed lands drained by the Mississippi River. They named it Louisiana in honor of their king. The land was later purchased from France by the United States in 1803. It was dubbed The Louisiana Purchase. Numerous states would later be created from these lands, one being Louisiana, which became a state in 1812.

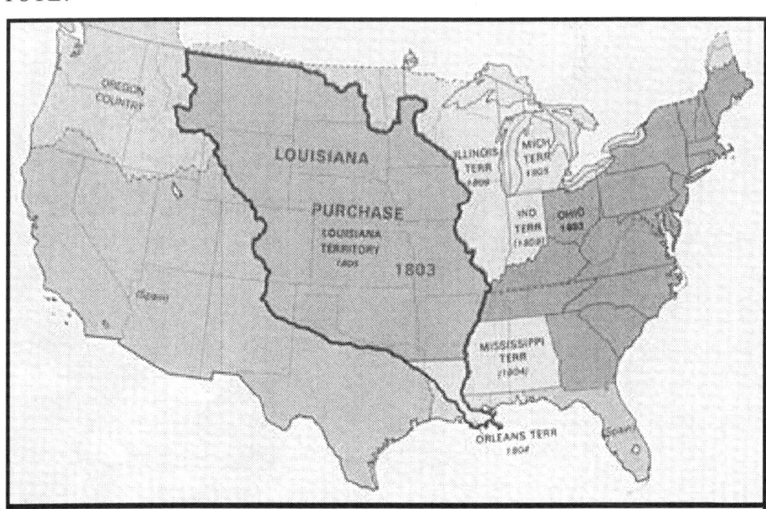

The Louisiana Purchase included land equaling approximately one-third of the continental United States.

Louis XV
(1710-1774)
He lived life to its fullest as a child

Louis XV

On August 26, 1715, the great Louis XIV was a dying man. As he lay on his death bed he sent for his great-grandson, then just five and a half years old. The boy was placed in an armchair beside the king's bed. The king turned his head. Tears filled his eyes as he looked at the boy for a moment. The boy sat up straight and looked directly to his great-grandfather. Reaching over to him, the king clasped the boy's hand. "One day you will become the greatest king in the world," he said. Then, staring directly into the boy's eyes, he added, "Never forget your fealty to God."

The king, letting go of the boy's hands, then raised his eyes and arms upwards, praying in a loud voice: "Lord, I offer him to Thee, this child. Grant him the favor to serve and honor Thee in a way worthy of a most Christian king and to make Thee adored and respected by all the peoples of his kingdom."

The little boy, frightened by the booming voice, burst into loud sobs after which he was hastily taken out of the room. Six days later Louis XIV died and the most remarkable reign in French history came to an end. The little boy (Louis XV) was now king of all France. This was so because at the age of two, Louis XV's father, mother, and brother all contracted diseases and died within one week, leaving him heir to the French throne.

It wasn't long afterwards that in Louis XV's copy-book were the words: "He who is born to reign must know that he is not destined for a quiet life in repose and pleasures, but rather to lead a laborious existence, subject to many perils."

The country in which Louis XV had inherited was in a state of poverty and disunion. The country had been plagued by prolonged wars, corrupt administrations, and religious quarrels. With the new king, the people cried out for change.

The Regent Philippe d'Orleans, however, would have the final say in matters of state until Louis turned thirteen. Louis XV, Philippe's great-nephew, would in turn concentrate on his lessons. In the process he did learn his kingly duties so much so that he was not content to play the part of a mere spectator in various court activities. He had read many times the instructions of Louis XIV which read, "Listen to the people. Seek advice from your councils, but decide alone."

On one occasion, a camp was set up and a mock battle staged. This was done about six miles from the palace at Versailles. The reason was so the young king (then about ten years old) could get more practical lessons in military art. Instead of watching the proceedings as was planned, Louis insisted on taking part and put himself at the head of the attacking army.

One of the king's early playmates, Marquis de Calviere, kept a journal of his experiences with the king. He wrote that the king (then eleven years old) led a normal life full of games and fun. Calviere wrote that the king when with people of his own age, behaved quite charmingly, showering gifts on his small companions. This included Easter eggs, a watch, copies of the Catechism, medals, a whip, balls, and other items.

Despite the fact, the king was quite frail as a boy; Calviere said the king and his friends often went on walks, outdoor excursions, and shrimping expeditions. They often would play soldiers or hopscotch. On a rainy day they would dress up, grate chocolate, and disassemble and reassemble mechanical toys. The young king also started to learn the art of dancing at the age of five and later liked to go hunting. He also enjoyed learning to operate a printing press and a lathe.

One day, Calviere wrote, the king was very sad. When asked what the problem was, the king said it was a toothache. The king, however, would not complain to the older people of the castle for fear they would take the tooth out and that would hurt.

Even at a very young age, the king had pretty much his own way. Nobody dared do much that would result in the king not liking them. So the king was permitted to do almost anything he liked. And he did just that. His favorite game was teasing, a trait which remained with him all his life. He enjoyed tiring his elderly tutor by long walks. He once hit his servant, threw some cheese at the head of one of the officials of the church, and even cut off the eyebrows from one of his court officers.

Because of the permissiveness, the king's education suffered. One observer noted that one of the king's books stayed open to the same page for six months. All of this was despite the fact the king had a team of instructors including some of the most learned men of letters, scientists, and mathematicians of the day. Although the king did enjoy geography and botany, he didn't have any great love for much else. Not acquiring a taste for study, there were few intellectual attainments.

He attended the Regency Council meetings regularly, however, the king didn't express much in the way of opinions. One minister said this: "At these meetings Louis opened his mouth, said little, and thought not at all."

His first real decision came when he was asked his opinion on a marriage that was being arranged for him with Anna-Maria Victoria of Spain, a girl who was then just three years old. Louis not only welcomed the arrangement but on her arrival presented her with an expensive gift.

This excited the new queen-to-be so much that she volunteered to kiss all the ministers who came to pay their respects. Although she did not fair that well through the various celebrations that were to follow, she did enjoy the fireworks. It was at the night spectacle that she kept tugging at the king's sleeve asking: "Monsieur! Monsieur! Is it not beautiful?"

"Oui," he answered.

Even at her young age, Anna-Maria Victoria was completely devoted to the king. Three years later (while still waiting to be married) she had an attack of the measles. Showing she intended to be an obedient wife, she refused help from the doctors until a file of guards brought an order from her "husband," the king.

Such devotion, however, was to no avail. The king, then fourteen years of age, was ready for marriage. The queen-to-be, however, was not yet eight years old, still much too young to bear children. The answer was to send the girl back to Spain and select another of marriageable age. The young girl did go back, later to became queen of Portugal.

The selection of a new queen for Louis was not all that easy. A list was made of all eligible girls of royal blood, twelve to twenty-five years of age. For some reason or another, all but one were rejected. The one selected was Marie Leczinska, the daughter of the deposed king of Poland. She was only added to the list as an afterthought with the notation, "There is nothing detrimental known concerning this family."

It was settled. Sight unseen the girl and the king agreed to the union. No sooner had the marriage plans been announced that a rumor spread throughout Paris that the new queen had webbed fingers and was both scrofulous and epileptic. The king immediately ordered a delegation of doctors to investigate the situation first hand. A message was sent back. The rumors were false. The new queen was perfectly normal.

At the time of their marriage the king was fifteen, the queen twenty-two. Though making no claim to beauty, the new queen was pleasant-looking, unselfish, and generous. There was little doubt that she would make a good wife and mother, an excellent choice for queen of France.

For a time the two lived as happily as most royal couples and she presented him with ten children in as many years. Neither partner, however, felt quite at ease with the other, though she respected his rank and he recognized her virtues. She did her duty to the best of her limited ability, but she could never be the friend and companion for whom he craved. Despite it all, and despite the tradition of immorality of past kings, at first Louis was true to his marriage vows to the surprise of everybody.

It wasn't to last. First there was the Duchess de Chateauroux and then Madame de Pompadour. When a fire took the life of the queen's father, there was no one left to love Marie Leczinska. For who but her father had counted even her tears as "jewels of infinite value?" Two years later she too died.

Louis XV paid his queen a last visit as she lay dead. He kissed her brow, perhaps remembering the bride who had come to him in a fever of gratitude.

Six years later the king too was on his death bed, a victim of smallpox. He asked for a last confession. After some thirty years of neglect, the confession took a total of sixteen minutes. Summarizing his career, the dying king said, "I governed and administrated badly because I had little talent and was ill-advised."

Today Louis XV has become best known for contributing to the decline of royal authority that led to the French Revolution in 1798. He had lost to the British nearly all of France's colonial possessions in North America and India. Not quite being labeled a failure as a king, one historian, Jerome Blum, said of Louis that he was "a perpetual adolescent called to do a man's job."

Louis XVII (1785-1795)
He was the little boy who was in the way

Louis XVII

Unlike the study of science where there are far more theories than fact, the study of history, it would seem, would be much more exact. Something either happened or it didn't happen. In most cases, this is true. Not so when you come to the story of the boy Louis XVII, who would have been king of France. His is a very unique story, a story that has caused historians a great deal of headaches over the years. It is best in this case to start not at the beginning, but at the end.

On a tombstone in Holland, there is the following inscription: "Here lies Louis XVII, Charles Louis, Duc de Normandie, King of France, and Navarre. Born at Versailles on March 27, 1785, deceased at Delft on August 10, 1845."

In France, one can find the following inscription on another tombstone. It reads: "Here lies Louis Charles of France. Son of Louis XVI and of Marie Antoninette. Born at Versailles on March 27, 1785, died at Gleize on August 10, 1853."

If that's not confusing enough, there is quite another record. In the archives of the Temple Section, City of Paris, there is the following: Temple Section. June 10, 1795. Louis Charles Capet, ten years two months old, son of Louis Capet, last King of the French, and of Marie Antoninette Josephe Jeanne of Austria. The deceased was born at Versailles, and died day before yesterday at three o'clock in the afternoon."

And there were other records, other tombstones, other graves. There is a grave with a boy's skeleton in it, in the moat of the Temple Tower in Paris. There are tombstones and graves in Westminster Abbey, Chicago, New York City, and in two other locations in France – all supposedly the last resting place of Louis XVII.

If the real boy king could stand up it would clear up one of the real mysteries of history. Since that more than likely won't occur, it evolves to the decision one must make of which story to believe.

Starting, however, at the beginning, what we do know is that the story of Louis XVII is the story of a boy who had everything and yet nothing, a boy who was in the way. In this, all historians agree.

Born March 27, 1785, in Versailles, France, Louis was the son of King Louis XVI and Queen Marie Antoinette. The timing of his birth wasn't good. Not only did his short life hang

Palace of Versailles

in the era of the French Revolution, but it was during the time when the monarchy was soon to be abolished. Neither rightly or wrongly his father was blamed for all of the nation's ills. As a consequence, the king was executed on January 21, 1793. At the time young Louis was just eight years old.

The boy, in fact, was never officially proclaimed king. Royalist supporters honored him as such, but due to the fact the nation was now proclaimed a republic, for better or worse, there would be no more members of the royalty recognized in France.

With turmoil all around him, young Louis tried to make the best of life. He was, after all, in his earlier years the king-to-be. So tutors at that time were busy during the day teaching him how to read and write. He was also taught manners, how to conduct himself in public, and greet people be they important emissaries or just common folks from the streets.

Before all the turmoil and in his spare time he enjoyed a small garden he had planted at the end of the terrace near the river. Here he would invite guards who were assigned to him, to join him. Sometimes children who lived nearby would come into it and talk to him. If they seemed very poor he would give them money.

Those better days, however, were short-lived. Soon outside the palace walls the French Revolution was about to begin. When it did, the royal family was kept virtual prisoners. Going outside the walls was most dangerous. It seemed no location was safe. One day the young Louis was taken prisoner. He was removed from the palace and imprisoned at a different location. Some stories said he

Marie Antoninette

was well taken care of, others said he was treated harshly. Nevertheless, French records reported that he had died on June 8, 1795. He was just ten years old. Two days later, records reported that he was buried, but no stone was erected to mark the spot.

All kinds of stories surfaced that the person buried was not Louis. Stories were told that he had escaped France and began a new life elsewhere. Years later several people claimed to be the grown-up Louis, some on their deathbed. Ultimately, as many as 100 "false dauphins" appeared over the years.

If you think this story couldn't get any stranger, well it did. It seems shortly after Louis had died in prison a doctor performed an autopsy. During the autopsy, as was often the custom, the boy's heart was removed and was not interred with the rest of the body. The doctor, instead, just kept it in a jar in his work room.

Knowing this, one of the doctor's students stole the heart. It was not known for years just who the culprit was or what happened to the heart. Then, on the former student's deathbed, he confessed. He told his wife to return it, but after he died she disobeyed him and gave the heart instead to the Archbishop of Paris. Here the heart stayed until the next revolution in 1830.

Then the heart went to Spain for a time and then to Austria. By 1975 it was back in France. It wasn't until 2000 when DNA testing was done. Results confirmed it was the heart of the boy king. That being the case, it was proved that the young king-to-be who was held in prison did not escape to live a life elsewhere. Due to the testing, it was also found that he in fact was directly related to Louis's mother, Marie Antoinette.

In a ceremony held June 8, 2004, the heart was finally buried next to the remains of Louis's parents. It was the first in over a century and most likely the last time that a royal ceremony would take place in France.

**The storming of the Bastille became
a symbol of the French Revolution (1789-1799).**

RUSSIA TODAY

CHAPTER 5
RUSSIA

Russia (now known as The Russian Federation) is today the largest country in the world, covering more than one eighth of the earth's inhabited land area. However, it does not lead in population. Eight other countries, including the most populous of all – India and China – hold that distinction.

What Russia does excel at is its long-held freezing winters. Much of the coastal areas are never entirely free of ice. The north is polar tundra and the southwest is chilly and arid. For this reason, most of the land is undesirable. Any farming throughout the country is difficult to produce and or maintain. Only in four small areas are there long and warm seasons.

Nevertheless, throughout Russia's long history, it has been a target for invasion. There is a lot of flat land and no towering mountain ranges to get in the way of an advancing army. Without natural barriers it was easy for armies from neighboring countries to come in to claim Russian land for their own. Although not well organized, the Russians stood their ground and held off those wishing them harm.

Among all the Russian tsars, there were only three who ruled while still children. Of these three, two became extremely internationally famous of all the monarchs of the world. This was Ivan IV, better known as Ivan the Terrible, Peter I, better known as Peter the Great, and Peter II.

In earlier times, Russia was but a group of scattered entities. It wasn't until 1547, when the first Tsar (Caesar) of Russia was crowned, that the country was transformed into a recognizable state. Thus began a period of rulers that lasted until the Russian Revolution of 1917. That's when the monarchy was abolished.

Ivan IV (Ivan the Terrible)
(1530-1584)
A terrible kid who did terrible things

Ivan IV

The sixteenth century was a time when much of Europe was reveling in the glories of the Renaissance. Russia was not. It was still struggling to establish its own identity. Then, to make matters worse, the country was presented with its first child ruler. That was the time when what was already bad got terribly worse. Meet Ivan IV.

It didn't help that his father, Basil, was under a curse when he was born. This curse, offered by the Patriarch of Jerusalem, was given because of Basil's disloyalty to the church's teachings. It read: "If you should do this wicked thing, you will have a wicked son; your states will become prey to terrors and tears; rivers of blood will flow; the heads of the mighty will fall; your cities will be devoured by flames..." Historians said that predictions that strong have a way to be remembered, particularly when they prove to be true.

Born in 1530, Ivan IV was but three years old when his father Basil died. Ivan's mother, Helken Glinska, proclaimed herself regent over her son. She successfully countered two throne-minded uncles with the help of her lover, Prince Ifan Obolensky. She even imprisoned them where they both died.

For her efforts, she was poisoned soon after in 1538. To cover up the crime after she became sick and then died, a funeral was held and she was buried all in a matter of hours. Her lover as well was then murdered to prevent any new protest. This gave the guardianship of the now orphaned boy ruler and control of the Russian government to others, the same who had killed his mother.

Still very young, Ivan well remembered what followed. On state occasions he was dressed in gorgeous robes and seated on his father's throne to welcome foreign ambassadors and to receive homage. This finished, the robes were laid aside and both he and his brother, Yuri, were then treated as menials, sent to their room, scorned, and deprived of food and clothing, all the while the royal treasury was being looted. During this time young Ivan was also constantly exposed to verbal and physical abuse. In those times, bloodshed, the killing off of one official after another, was commonplace in scrambles for power.

For his education, Ivan was often taken to the torture chambers and to executions; for that, his teachers said, was part of what he needed to know as a ruler. It was a cruel age, not only in Russia, but in many other parts of the world as well.

Rather than rejecting such behavior, Ivan, even as a young boy, seemed to behave just as badly. Unable to strike out at his tormentors he took his frustrations out on defenseless animals. He would tear off the feathers of birds while they were still alive. He also would, just for fun, haul cats and dogs to the top of the Kremlin towers and then fling them off to their death on the ground below.

This love of doing bad things wasn't centered just on animals. Still very young, Ivan also liked to mount his horse and go galloping through Moscow's streets, knocking down old men and women without any regard to persons or property. He enjoyed robbing and beating up farmers. He started drinking heavily and by the age of ten was often so drunk he couldn't walk. Nobody in his household cared what he did. As far

A portion of the Kremlin wall.

as they were concerned, he was out of the way and didn't interfere in what evil deeds they were doing.

Little did they know that what Ivan was doing to others, he would soon be doing to them. That came to pass when Ivan became thirteen years old. He told himself that now was the time to take full control of the government and to do revenge on those who were acting badly in his name.

He told his guards, staking everything on their loyalty, to arrest the person in power at the time, the ruthless Prince Andrew Shuisky. They did so and, on Ivan's orders, put him to death. Many others of the court who were now expendable were also arrested and either imprisoned or put to death as well. Some thirty offending individuals followed these. Ivan gave orders that they be strung up on gallows. For Ivan, it was all good.

His only wish now was to be crowned officially, not as Grand Prince, but as tsar. He also wanted to be married, not to some foreign princess for political purposes, but to a Russian girl of his selection. At age sixteen, that is just what happened. Ivan, now free from those who controlled him, contin-

158

ued to do his will.

One such misadventure came shortly after when, hearing of a secret treasure located at the Cathedral of St. Sophia, he went into the church late at night and tortured those in charge until at last he uncovered a chest loaded with silver bullion. This he loaded on carts and sent it to Moscow.

As he grew older, he trusted no one. He would not go out among the people. He spent most of his time in solitude. He was often touched with madness. Given to rages and paranoia, he even killed his own son during an argument.

His involvement in the Massacre of Novgorod is regarded as one of his biggest demonstrations of his mental instability and brutality. Here in 1570 and just on the hunch the citizens were betraying him, he tortured and killed several thousand citizens. Even women and children of all ages were included. They were bound and thrown in the icy river to drown.

For those who thought of him as being a terrible man who did terrible things, he lived up to his name – Ivan the Terrible. His end came in 1584, a heart attack while playing chess. He was fifty-six years old, dying not soon enough for most of Russia. What he left was a country in disarray with deep political and social scars.

**Early artist rendition of the
1570 Massacre of Novgorod.**

Peter I

Peter I (Peter the Great)
(1672-1725)
One of the world's greatest leaders

If you visit Moscow, Russia, today you will find a large building on Red Square called the Kremlin Armory. Here is the nation's oldest museum. Founded in 1808, the museum houses the Imperial Crown of Russia, carriages, and furniture used by the nation's earliest rulers. Two of the artifacts on display are actual thrones, one used by Ivan the Terrible and the other by Peter the Great.

The Peter the Great throne is different in one way in the fact it is not just one throne, but two, joined together. It also has a large round hole in the back. The hole was the brainchild of his older half-sister, Sophia. Soon after the death of her father, Tsar Fyedor, Sophia was named regent to her younger brothers, the joint kings Ivan V, then age sixteen, and his ten-year-old younger brother Peter I, later to be known as Peter the Great.

The joint throne was where the young rulers would sit on formal occasions, dressed in stiff robes of state. Both held a globe and scepter and greeted all who entered. These included nobles who often asked favors of the rulers, statesmen offering advice, and foreign ambassadors presenting their credentials. It was customary as well for the new rulers to confirm the treaties made by their predecessors. Often questions would be asked and the young rulers would be expected to answer these questions.

Because the young tsars were not fully prepared to offer them, Sophia would help. Unbeknownst to the visitors, she had this large hole cut into the back of the throne chair where she would, out of sight, whisper the answers she expected them to offer. After these formal audiences, the visitors often went away amazed at the intelligent answers the boys gave.

It was the younger boy Peter who was alert to the questions

Ivan V

and answered most of them. His brother Ivan was not only half blind, but lame and feeble-minded. While Peter sat erect in his chair, his alert brown eyes continually looking about, Ivan was slouching in his chair, staring at the limp hands in his lap. Regardless, the two brothers always got along great and neither had a problem sharing the responsibilities.

Due to his chronic illnesses, Ivan wasn't expected to live long. For a while he fooled everyone, got married, and had several children. Eventually his illnesses caught up with him. He died in 1686 at the age of twenty-nine. The boy Peter, twenty-three years old at the time, was now officially sole ruler of Russia. Unofficially that was the case years before due to Ivan's inability to govern.

To take over as sole ruler, Peter was well qualified. When his father was still alive he would take his young son with him on official visits and ceremonies. Peter had his own small carriage drawn by four ponies and driven by dwarfs. He was highly popular among the people along the way.

Even after his father had died, the boy, growing up, was active in his studies, welcoming knowledge in all things. He even found ways to turn what he was learning into practical use while he was playing. With his playmates he organized them into sort of a military school and learned with them all what was necessary to form an army. Together, with the help of tutors, they studied fortification. They learned the use of tools, problem solving, drilling, marching, and working as a team.

In all of this Peter was not leading, but being a part of the group. In his adventures about the countryside he found an English sailboat, which was derelict in a shed. With some help he fixed it up, got it seaworthy, and

Russian Cossack rider.

practiced sailing. This whetted his passion for seafaring.

All of this prepared him for leading his country, which he did well. In later life he expanded his kingdom through a number of successful wars. He replaced the old way of doing things with modern ones. He built a large navy, established colleges, and got rid of arranged marriages, long practiced by nobles. All of this made a lasting impact on Russia and the institutions that governed it. When he died in 1725 he was fifty-two years old, having reigned forty-two years.

Peter II (1715-1730)
Orphaned at age three,
died on his wedding day, age fourteen

Peter II

For many who lived in earlier times, life was short. For rulers or soon-to-be rulers often it was even shorter. That was because power-hungry individuals were not immune to killing off all those blood relatives who stood in their way, although murder wasn't always necessary. Plans often got changed due to a common occurrence during those times which was disease. Any disease was often fatal due to the limited ways to cure even common ailments. Such was the case for Peter II of Russia.

Peter's mother, Princess Charlotte, died while giving birth to him. Then, at age three, Peter got the news that his father, the Tsarevich Alexis, was executed, accused of treason. Because of the boy's age, father and son barely got to know each other. Peter, now an orphan, was turned over to strangers.

There was an extended succession of folks, in fact, many who treated Peter harshly. Among these was Prince Menshikov who at this time had the power in the court. He dashed Peter to his own estates, away from the Kremlin. Menshikov even tried to marry Peter off, then just eleven years old, to his daughter Maria. Peter, however, didn't like Maria and so he appealed to friends and his sister for help. It took some time but help came and Menshikov and his family were exiled to Siberia.

Now, back at the Kremlin, Peter was presented with a new tutor. A Hungarian refugee, a teacher who actually did his job. He got Peter involved in history, geography, mathematics, and science. Peter even learned to understand German, French, and Latin. Unfortunately Peter was not a good student. His teacher said at the time that while Peter was naturally intelligent and had a good heart, he was stubborn.

Instead of learning, he preferred to go hunting or indulging in the rich foods prepared in the palace kitchens. When not in class Peter became totally engrossed in various amusements that included card playing. He even got himself addicted to alcohol.

For a brief moment, he did seem to be interested in his official coronation on January 9, 1728. For eleven-year-old Peter it was, in fact, a lavish affair with a huge entourage. Rather than being awestruck at the ceremonies, observers said he was mostly disengaged. Then, when expected at council meetings to make decisions, he often just wouldn't show up. The last thing he wanted to think about was national affairs. He had no desire to rule and this at a time when it was needed most.

Foreign witnesses reported that it was a time when all of Russia was in terrible disorder. Money was not being paid to anyone. They said that everyone was stealing as much as they could. Even when Peter was presented with the news that the Russian fleet was in dire straits, Peter responded that he had no interest in the sea and didn't want to discuss the matter.

He did, however, get interested when marriage was mentioned. That was after Peter, at age fourteen, became smitten with eighteen-year-old Ekaterina Dolgorukou. After their engagement and while on her way to the palace things just didn't go that well. The king's carriage, in which she was riding, got stuck in a rut. Then, the golden crown atop the carriage fell off and smashed onto the ground. Many regarded this as a bad omen.

They may have been right. In the days to follow, after plans were made and all was ready for a big wedding, the king was not. But this time it was not from a lack of interest. Earlier in that week Peter was outside in the cold weather reviewing his troops. He became ill and that illness soon turned into smallpox. On the actual day he was to be married, he died. He was just fourteen years old. As a ruler, young Peter hadn't done much. But for some reason he was buried in the Kremlin, the only Russian monarch given that honor.

Cathedral of the Archangel in the Kremlin complex– burial place of Peter II.

ABOUT THE AUTHOR

Joe Kraus spent his high school years in Salem Oregon and was voted most likely to succeed in his North Salem High School journalism class. That was all the encouragement he needed. His first national magazine article was published while he was still in high school. And after his military service and going to college, he ended up as a managing editor on several daily newspapers. Since then some 300 articles has followed, published in more than 60 different national periodicals.

He has founded two national magazines, *Autograph Collector Magazine* and *Child Stars* Magazine, both now are no longer published. This gave more time to focus on his non-fiction books. Joe's first book, *Alive in the Desert*, published in 1978, was used in the popular TV series Air Wolf starring Ernest Borgnine. A revised edition of the book *Staying Alive In The Desert: The Complete Guide To Desert Survival* was released April 2017. Other books released to date are *Desert Rats: They Came With A Pick, A Shovel And A Dream* and *The Famous & Successful: Their Advice For All Of Us* that was co-written by Ron Stovall.

Married to his wife, Karren for nearly 50 years, they have three grown children Heidi Delaney, Peter Kraus, and Rebecca Sprinkle and six grandchildren Jaycee Henson, Shawn Kraus, Caitlyn Sprinkle, Joshua Sprinkle, Addyson Sprinkle, and Carter Sprinkle.

Made in the USA
Columbia, SC
31 December 2017